Introduction

All recommendations and advice in this book come from my own research and experiences traveling in Morocco (the information in the rebook is updated every year).

The guide is designed in this way:

- Easy to read, with lots of illustrations and photographs so that you have inspiration for choosing your travel destinations.
- The guide's aim is that, in a reading time of only 1 hour, you will have a general idea of how to travel to Morocco. This way, you save time and research effort.
- It is a guide that summarizes in a straightforward style all the basics for your trip to Morocco.
- The book contains affiliate links. These links provide me with a small commission if you purchase through them (but at no cost to you).

I am Alberto Barambio Canet, a passionate traveler from Llombai (Valencia), Spain.

I taveled around Morocco for 1 month: I started from the North (Tangier), passing through all the destinations that I recommend in the guide.

With it, you will be able to plan your trip in a faster and easier way, in just 1 hour of reading.

The guide aims to inspire you with numerous photographs of the best destinations in Morocco. It also informs you about all the basics you need for your trip.

So get ready to get to know the most fashionable and popular country for people venturing to Africa.

These are the things that fascinated me the most about Morocco:

1. The diversity in its destinations: blue villages, deserts, remote towns among mountains, modern cities and coastal towns.

2. The interesting and rich Islamic culture.

3. Morocco is the best country to start traveling in Africa: it is safe and has good communications, and infrastructure compared to other surrounding countries.

4. Its gastronomy: they have delicious typical dishes.

Finally, I would like to encourage you to say hello to me on Instagram. I will be happy to answer any questions you may have about your next trip to Morocco or suggestions on how to improve the guide.

1 HOUR TRAVEL GUIDES

✉ ABARAMBIO1@GMAIL.COM

f 1HOURTRAVELGUIDES

📷 @1HOURTRAVELGUIDES

➤ LINKTR.EE/1HOURTRAVELGUIDES

Index

Before your trip

A bit of history

about Morocco

1 GEOGRAPHY AND HERITAGE

Due to its strategic location in northwest Africa, Morocco has been home to several civilizations. Its landscape is very varied: from the Rif and Atlas Mountains, to the extensive Atlantic and Mediterranean coastline, which has influenced its history and culture.

2 ANCIENT CIVILIZATIONS

The Phoenicians established colonies on the north coast, followed by the Carthaginians and Romans. The region was also home to Mauritanians, Vandals and Visigoths. Despite these influences, the Berbers have persisted over time in Morocco to this day, pre-serving their culture and language.

3 ISLAMIZATION AND DYNASTY

In the 7th century, Islam arrived with the Arab conquest and the introduction of the Idrisid dynasty. During the following centuries, the Almohad and Marinid dynasties flourished, leaving their mark on architecture and culture.

4 ARAB AND OTTOMAN INFLUENCE

The rise of the Saadian dynasty marked the unification of the country in the 16th century. But Arab influence and Ottoman intervention in the 17th century brought about political and social changes.

5 FRENCH AND SPANISH PROTECTORATE

At the beginning of the 20th century, Morocco was divided into zones of French and Spanish influence. This period of protectorate led to many tensions, such as the resistance led by Mohammed V and Mohammed Ben Aarafa.

6 INDEPENDENCE

In 1956, Morocco gained independence and Mohammed V became king. His successor, Hassan II, played a key role in the modernization of the country.

ESSAOUIRA

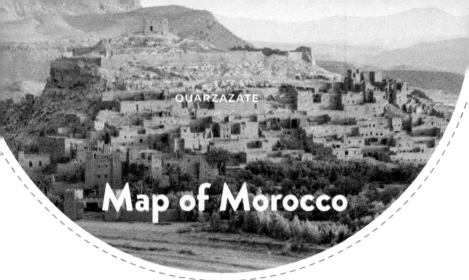

OUARZAZATE

Map of Morocco

Below you can scan the Google map QR code with
all my recommendations in Morocco. The map is
automatically copied once you save it in your account.

Destinations

Restaurants

Places of interest

Transportation

**How to download the free map from Google Maps to
your phone:**

1) Open Google Maps.
2) In the search bar type "Okay maps".
3) Select the city or area and click on "download".

Morocco

Inspiration
for your trip

Movies

CASABLANCA
Michael Curtiz

HORSES OF GOD
Nabil Ayouch

CASANEGRA
Nour-Eddine
Lakhmari

MAROCK
Laïla Marrakchi

Books

THE TRAVELS OF IBN
BATTUTAH
Ibn Battutah

IN ARABIAN NIGHTS
Tahir Shah

MY 1001 NIGHTS
Alice Morrison

Music

TRAVEL MOROCCO Spotify
QR Code

Did you know that...?

FOREIGN COUPLES CAN SLEEP TOGETHER IN HOTELS
However, Moroccans and even Arab foreigners often need a marriage certificate.

SPAIN AND EUROPE ARE LOCATED ONLY 15 KM AWAY FROM Morocco. From Tangier you can perfectly see Spain through the Strait of Gibraltar.

MOROCCO HAS THE OLDEST UNIVERSITY IN THE WORLD.
which has been operating continuously since its foundation). It is called "Al-Qarawiyyin" and was founded in 859 in Fes.

THE ATLAS LION IS THE NATIONAL ANIMAL.
It is extinct in the wild, but there are still specimens in zoos and circuses.

IN MOROCCO THE HEART DOES NOT SYMBOLIZE LOVE.
The liver is the organ that traditionally represents desire and love.

Did you know that...?

MOROCCO HAS 4 IMPERIAL CITIES: Rabat, Fes, Meknes and Marrakech. All of them have been capitals of Morocco at some point in its history.

ITS OFFICIAL LANGUAGES ARE ARABIC AND BERBER. Although the use of French is common and part of the population speaks Spanish and English.

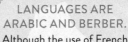

PLUG TYPE: C&E The standard voltage is **220 V** and the frequency is **50 Hz.**

MOROCCO IS ONE OF THE 11 COUNTRIES WHERE THE SAHARA IS LOCATED. The desert is the largest and hottest in the world.

MOUNT TOUBKAL is the highest mountain in Morocco and the second highest in Africa at 4,167m.

ESSAOUIRA

📖 **Vocabulary** in Morocco

There are some terms that you will hear constantly in Morocco and maybe you won't know what they mean. In this page I explain their meaning:

1 Souk: they are traditional markets or bazaars. They are organized in specialized sections such as the perfume souk, the jewelry souk or the clothing souk.

2 Medina: is the old and historical part of the city. It is characterized by narrow alleys, markets and historic buildings.

3 Riad: traditional Moroccan house, usually located in the medinas, which have a large inner courtyard or garden.

4 Dar: similar to a riad, but a little smaller.

5 Kasbah: fortress or citadel, built of abode or mud bricks and surrounded by high walls.

6 Ksar: fortified village or town. It is made of mud or adobe and has high defensive walls. They are usually found in arid and desert regions. The most important ksar in Morocco is Ait Ben-Haddou.

7 Corniche: of French origin, it is used to refer to the promenade.

8 Hammam: a kind of Moroccan-style spa. Locals usually go to a hammam at least once a week. You can find public or private ones.

9 Madrassa: school where the Koran is taught.

10 Jalaba: typical Berber piece of clothing. It is a long tunic with a hood.

11 Hijab: headscarf worn by many women.

Weather
and best times to visit

 **CLIMATE IN MOROCCO**

Morocco has a pleasant climate all year round. These are some of its general characteristics:

- Coastal cities have a good climate from January to December.
- It hardly rains throughout the year in the country.
- The best months for swimming are from June to October.
- Cities near the Atlas Mountains and the desert are usually cold during The winter and very hot in summer.
- The months with best weather are: April-June, September-October.
- The months with more tourists: April, July, August, October and December.

ATLANTIC COAST
- Pleasant temperatures all year round.
- It can be very windy: that's why surfing and kitesurfing are popular on this coast.
- The water temperature is freezing during the winter.

ATLAS AND SAHARA
- Cold during the winter months. It can even snow in the Atlas Mountains.
- Very hot during the summer.
- Climate with hardly any rainfall.

MARRAKECH/FEZ
- Very warm climate in the summer and cold mornings and evenings in the winter.
- Pleasant temperatures fo the rest of the year.

TANGIER/CHEFCHAOUEN
- Cold weather during the mornings and evenings in the winter.
- Pleasant temperatures during most of the year.

DESTINATIONS	JAN	FEB	MAR	APR	MAY	JUN	JUL	AUG	SEP	OCT	NOV	DEC
Tangier	14°C/109MM	14°C/98MM	17°C/106MM	17°C/73MM	20°C/31MM	23°C/0MM	24°C/0MM	25°C/0MM	22°C/25MM	22°C/86MM	17°C/99MM	15°C/99MM
Chefchaouen	13°C/95MM	13°C/84MM	14°C/89MM	16°C/63MM	19°C/33MM	22°C/10MM	24°C/3MM	25°C/9MM	20°C/28MM	17°C/94MM	15°C/132MM	15°C/71MM
Fes-Meknes	11°C/85MM	13°C/92MM	15°C/109MM	20°C/78MM	26°C/49MM	31°C/16MM	35°C/0MM	34°C/28MM	29°C/44MM	20°C/65MM	15°C/94MM	13°C/61MM
Merzhouga	12°C/7MM	14°C/7MM	18°C/17MM	23°C/10MM	26°C/16MM	31°C/9MM	35°C/11MM	34°C/17MM	25°C/26MM	24°C/1MM	17°C/9MM	13°C/5MM
Quarzazate	10°C/6MM	12°C/17MM	15°C/13MM	18°C/3MM	23°C/10MM	26°C/6MM	30°C/5MM	29°C/11MM	25°C/15MM	20°C/13MM	15°C/6MM	11°C/5MM
Marrakech	15°C/33MM	16°C/38MM	18°C/48MM	20°C/30MM	23°C/24MM	26°C/6MM	30°C/0MM	31°C/0MM	26°C/23MM	25°C/18MM	20°C/31MM	16°C/22MM
Taghazout Essaouira	31°C/109MM	43°C/109MM	33°C/109MM	15°C/109MM	18°C/109MM	22°C/0MM	24°C/0MM	25°C/6MM	24°C/6MM	22°C/10MM	19°C/33MM	17°C/31MM
Casablanca	15°C/90MM	15°C/71MM	16°C/77MM	18°C/50MM	21°C/34MM	23°C/9MM	25°C/5MM	26°C/12MM	24°C/18MM	23°C/50MM	19°C/125MM	17°C/65MM
Rabat	14°C/63MM	14°C/48MM	16°C/49MM	17°C/36MM	21°C/24MM	23°C/9MM	24°C/4MM	25°C/10MM	24°C/23MM	22°C/43MM	20°C/31MM	16°C/42MM

Best weather • Ok • Less favorable | North • Sahara • Center • Coast

IMPORTANT DATES

- <u>Ramadan:</u> lasts 30 days. In 2024 it starts on March 11. During these days, many places close and life is slower in Morocco.

- <u>Prayer times:</u> in Morocco there are 5 prayer times: Fajr (before sunrise), Zuhr (noon), Asr (after noon), Maghrib (afternoon-evening), and Isha (night).

You will notice that the mosques use megaphones with a very loud volume that can be heard throughout the city.

Prayer times are adjusted throughout the year according to the position of the sun.

- <u>Opening hours:</u> life in general, stores, museums and markets are usually open from 9 am. At noon there are establishments that close for siesta. And the closing time of museums and attractions is usually around 5 pm.

- <u>Friday:</u> life is slower and some places close as it is a sacred day.

TIME CHANGE

Since 2018, Morocco changes the time from UTC+0 to UTC+1. They change the clocks according to the dates of Ramadan instead of winter and summer time.

Thus, night time comes earlier and facilitates the fasting of Ramadan.

In 2024:

- On March 10, at 3:00 am the clock is changed to 2:00 am.

- On April 14, at 2:00 am the time is changed to 3:00 am.

DAY	HOLIDAY
01/01/2024	New Year's Day
11/01/2024	Independence Manifesto
10/04/2024	Eid Al-Fitr
01/05/2024	Labor Day
17/06/2024	Islamic Feast of Sacrifice
08/07/2024	Islamic New Year
30/07/2024	Coronation of the King

DAY	HOLIDAY
14/08/2024	Western Sahara Day
20/08/2024	Revolution Day
21/08/2024	Youth Day
16/09/2024	Prophet's Birthday
06/11/2024	Green March Anniversary
18/11/2024	Independence Day
21/12/2024	Winter Solstice

Preparations
for the trip

VISA

Many countries do NOT require visas to enter Morocco. Among them: USA, Canada, Great Britain, most European countries and some Latin American countries.

In this link you can see the countries that do need to apply for a visa and what are the requirements: **https://visaguide.world/africa/morocco-visa/**

WHAT ARE THE REQUIREMENTS TO ENTER MOROCCO AS A TOURIST?

1. Passport valid for more than 6 months
2. Medical insurance.
3. Proof of first accommodation in the country (hotel address, Airbnb or acquaintances).
4. A ticket out of the country.

*Points 2, 3 and 4 may not be checked at immigration.

If you do not have a clear date of return or departure from Morocco, you can use the 'Onward Ticket' service: this company reserves you a flight ticket that lasts 1-2 days. It serves as proof of return to pass the immigration control.

TETOUAN

ONWARD FLIGHT

MORE INFORMATION

- How many days can I stay in Morocco as a tourist? 90 days.
- Cost for citizens who do not need a tourist visa: free entry.
- You receive an entry stamp in your passport.

MUST-HAVE APPLICATIONS ON YOUR PHONE

•Careem/InDrive

Street cabs may not want to put the meter on and charge you an abusive price. Especially in Marrakech.

So, I recommend the use one of these 2 apps to order a cab.

The only drawback is that the waiting time is usually high.

•Google Maps/Maps.me

Very useful to move easily in your destinations. Download the maps of Morocco to use it in offline places.

•Splitwise

Great application if you travel in company. It helps you to keep track of your trip and split expenses.

•Google Translator

You can easily survive in Morocco if you speak Arabic, French, Spanish or English. But if you have difficulty communicating, the use of this application is common in Morocco.

WIFI

Wifi internet connection in Morocco is good. Airbnbs, hotels, hostels and cafés have connections. During my stay in Morocco I was able to make video calls without any problems.

SIM CARD

In Morocco there is a good data signal almost everywhere in the country: the connection is usually stable and fast (even sometimes between mountains and in the Sahara).

You can get SIM cards at:

- The airport upon arrival.
- Kiosks.
- Phone providers stores (as mentioned below).

The 3 companies in Morocco are:

- Maroc Telecom.
- Orange.
- Inwi.

Points to consider:

- SIM card price: ($2).
- Price Gb: $1/1Gb approx.
- The company with the best connection is Maroc Telecom and the worst Inwi.

ESIM

eSIMs have a more expensive data connection than local cards. However, they are a good option if:

- You make a short trip.
- If you run out of data.
- Want to guarantee a fast connection.

The one I use on my trips is from AIRALO.

TRAVEL INSURANCE

Although it is uncommon to be asked to show it, travel insurance is a mandatory requirement to enter Morocco.

Very important to travel with insurance, and although trips usually go well, you never know when you might have an accident or require hospital care.

Don't ruin your vacation because of a huge doctor's bill or avoid going to the hospital when you need to because you don't have insurance.

The ones I have used in my years of world travel are:

- SafetyWing: although they target digital nomads on the web, their product is travel insurance.
- IATI: they have a wide variety of insurances for families, backpackers or even for more expensive countries like USA or Japan. You have a 5% discount with my code.
- WorldTrips: one of the most reputable companies in travel insurance and one of the oldest in the market.

VACCINATIONS

Although there are no mandatory vaccinations to enter Morocco, the World Health Organization recommends the following:

- Hepatitis A
- Hepatitis B
- Varicella (chicken pox)
- Influenza
- Rabies
- Measles
- TDAP (Tetanus, diphtheria and pertussis)
- MMR (Meningitis, mumps and rubella)
- Typhoid fever

*Beware of mosquitoes: there are no cases of malaria in Morocco, but there are cases of dengue fever.

RECOMMENDATIONS WHEN EATING

Beware of diarrhea in these situations:

- Drinking tap water.
- Ice in drinks.
- When eating salads and fruits.

You can eat more safely if:

- The water has been boiled.
- When the food is cooked and not raw.

BATHROOMS

In Morocco you will not find much luxury in the bathrooms and they are usually not very clean.

Do not expect to find public toilets either. As a general rule, the toilets have seats. However, in the country side and in rural areas, it is common to find squat toilets.

It is very important to bring handkerchiefs, wipes or your own toilet paper, since you won't find them everywhere.

Keep in mind these tips for packing your suitcase:

1) Check the weather: although Morocco has a pleasant climate almost all year round, you may need:

- Warm clothes if you are traveling to the Sahara or Atlas Mountains, for chilly nights or if you are visiting in the winter.
- Beach clothes if you go to the coast or plan to surf.
- Summer clothes: most of the year it is hot in Morocco.

2) Appropriate footwear:

- Flip flops for the Beach or shower.
- Comfortable shoes for walking around your destination.
- Hiking shoes if you go to the Atlas Mountains.

3) Sunscreen and repellent: You will need sunscreen, as Morocco has a sunny climate all year round. Also don't forget mosquito repellent.

4) Adapter: It is important to bring an adapter to be able to connect your electronic devices. To avoid complicating your life, I recommend you to buy a universal adapter: it is more expensive, but you can use it in any country in the world.

5) Travel backpack: my preference for travel is to always go with a 55-liter backpack. I can always carry it as cabin luggage and it's easier to transport by carrying it on your back.

Anyway, I also leave you another very good option of a sturdy and quality wheeled suitcase. You can see all these products in the QR code below.

6) Money/credit cards:

- I recommend that you travel with at least, 2 credit cards for 2 reasons: they can get stolen or get damaged or misplaced.
- It is also advisable to travel with the cards in different places in your luggage in case you get robbed.
- It is advisable to travel with a money belt to keep cash and one of the cards.

DON'T FORGET:

- That your passport is valid for 6 months.
- Organize and store your travel documents in an easily accessible place.
- Download and test phone applications before leaving.
- Always carry this book with you.

My travel products

List

TRAVEL ESSENTIALS

» Backpack or suitcase
» Backpack for day trips
» Money belt
» Microfiber towel
» Flip flops
» Walking shoes
» Universal adapter
» Padlock

DOCUMENTS

» Passport
» Wallet
» Credit or debit card
» Travel insurance
» Copy of important documents

ELECTRONIC PRODUCTS

» Camera and memory cards
» External battery
» Phone
» Chargers

CLOTHING

» Clothing
» Cap/hat
» Sweatshirt
» 1 piece of coat
» Long pants
» Shorts
» Short sleeve T-shirt
» Underwear
» 1 dress/skirt
» Swimsuit
» Sunglasses
» Belt

PERSONAL HYGIENE PRODUCTS

» Sunscreen
» Mosquito repellent
» Antibacterial gel
» Deodorant
» Toothbrush and toothpaste
» Shaving razor
» Feminine hygiene products
» Paracetamol
» Diarrhea tablets

PREPARE YOUR TRIP

Space for you to plan your trip: what you need to bring in your luggage, write down your flights, hotel reservations or places you plan to visit.

Itineraries

Tangier

Chefchaouen

Casablanca

Rabat

Fes

Meknes

Marrakech

Essaouira

Taghazout

Ouarzazate

Sahara
(Merzouga)

MOROCCO

Zones of Morocco

Before talking about itineraries, you should know the most common ways to enter Morocco:

- <u>Plane:</u> all the destinations I recommend (except Chefchaoen), have an airport nearby.
- <u>Ferry:</u> You can cross by boat from Spain to Tangier.

For a better organization, I like to divide the recommended destinations in these zones:

1. NORTH
(Tangier, Chefchaoen, Meknes and Fes).

2. SAHARA
(Merzouga)

3. CENTRAL PART
(Ouarzazate, Marrakech).

4. ATLANTIC COAST
(Essaouira, Taghazout, Casablanca and Rabat).

1 week itinerary
(North Morocco Route)

Do this route if you start your trip from the north of Morocco in Tangier or from Fez, and you do not have much time.

DAY 1-3 ▸ TANGIER

DAY 4-5 ▸ CHEFCHAOUEN

DAY 6-7 ▸ FES

MARRAKECH

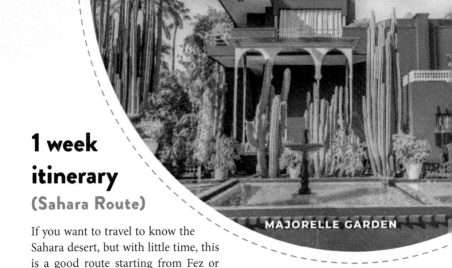

MAJORELLE GARDEN

1 week itinerary
(Sahara Route)

If you want to travel to know the Sahara desert, but with little time, this is a good route starting from Fez or Marrakech.

DAY 1-2 ▸ FES

DAY 3-4 ▸ MERZOUGA DESERT

DAY 5 ▸ OUARZAZATE

DAY 6-7 ▸ MARRAKECH

1 week itinerary
(Atlantic Ocean Route)

Perfect route if your flight arrives as far as Agadir, Casablanca or Rabat and you want to see destinations in the Atlantic Ocean.

DAY 1-2 ▸ FES

DAY 3-4 ▸ MERZOUGA DESERT

DAY 5 ▸ OUARZAZATE

DAY 6-7 ▸ MARRAKECH

12 days itinerary
(Imperial Cities and desert route)

If you are looking to see the 4 imperial cities (former capitals of Morocco), the Sahara desert and some Moroccan must-sees such as the Kasbah Aït-Ben-Haddou in Ouarzazate and the Hassan II Mosque in Casablanca.

DAY 1 ▸ MEKNES

DAY 2-3 ▸ FES

DAY 4-5 ▸ MERZOUGA

DAY 6 ▸ OUARZAZATE

DAY 6-9 ▸ MARRAKECH

DAY 10 ▸ CASABLANCA

DAY 10-11 ▸ RABAT

3 weeks itinerary
(All destinations)

This is the route that I did in my trip to Morocco in which you will be able to know all the destinations that I recommend. Only for travelers who really want to know Morocco in depth.

MARRAKECH

BEN YOUSSEF MADRASA

KOUTUBIA MOSQUE

Destinations

Tangier

RECOMMENDED DAYS
2-3

In Tangier you can experience a unique fusion of Arabic, French and Spanish culture. Its narrow streets in the medina refl ect the Moorish influence, while its buildings and squares show the European past.

This city is located only 15 km from Spain, which can be clearly seen from the viewpoints of Tangier.

Get to know this city walking through its medina, and knowing the kasbah to have the best views of the Mediterranean.

INSTAGRAM

TANGIER
DE @1HOURTRAVELGUIDES

Medina | Gastronomy

↑ Here you will find

Things to do:
Tangier

1   MEDINA

The historic center of Tangier is not as large and chaotic as others in Morocco. There you can find a multitude of restaurants, stores and narrow alleys where most of the accommodations are located.

2   HAFA COFFEE

This café, founded in 1920, is located on a cliff overlooking the Strait of Gibraltar.

It is a typical place for locals to go to drink tea, coffee and to watch the sunset.

In addition, Tangier has several traditional cafés that are well worth a visit. Go to: "Grand Café de Paris", "Café a l'Anglaise" and "Grand Café Central.

3   CAVES OF HERCULES

They are located 14 km west of Tangier. The cave has 2 entrances: one by land and the other by sea. This one is said to have the shape of the African continent.

Mythology says that the god Hercules stayed and slept in this cave.

4   BEACHES

Tangier has some good sandy beaches near the city. The best are "Dalia", "Ba Kacem" and "Playa Blanca".

5   IBN BATUTTA MUSEUM

A must-see museum to get to know one of the largest museums in the world. travelers of history.

Ibn Batutta traveled for more than 120,000 km on foot and by boat in the 14th century (even more than Marco Marco Polo). The museum recounts his his travels in North Africa, the Middle East and Asia.

📍 Borj Naam

🕐 8 am-10 pm, Fri-Wed

💲 $3

6   KASBAH

Do not miss the opportunity to visit the fortress of Tangier. There you can visit the Kasbah Museum and have nice views of the Strait of Gibraltar.

Things to do: Tangier

7 KASBAH MUSEUM

It displays artifacts from the civilizations that populated the area from prehistoric times to the 19th century. A highlight is the exhibition of the Roman mosaic found in Volubilis.

📍 Place de la Kasbah

🕐 10am-6 pm, Tue-Sun

💲 $2

8 9 APRIL 1947 SQUARE

One of the most atmospheric spots in the city. I recommend visiting by sunset time. Local people gather to chat and taste street food. I also recommend you to visit the Cinema Rif, which is located in the square and stands out for its art deco architecture.

9 CONTINENTAL HOTEL

The hotel opened its doors in 1870, where famous writers and artists have passed through. Stop by for a coffee, admire its architecture and have great views of the Strait of Gibraltar.

📍 36 Rue Dar-el-Baroud

10 CAPE SPARTEL LIGHTHOUSE

Visit the lighthouse that marks the division of the Atlantic Ocean and the Mediterranean Sea, located on a cliff.
This beautiful white lighthouse is located 15 km from Tangier.

11 TETOUAN

This beautiful village is located only 60 km from Tangier. Many travelers take advantage of their stay in Tangier to make a day trip to Tetouan. It stands out for its beautiful medina with white painted houses.

TETOUAN

Tours in Tangier

1 DAY TOUR TO CHEFCHAOUEN

Get to know the blue city on a day trip from Chefchaouen.

SUNSET CAMEL RIDE

Visit the lighthouse of Tangier, Hercules caves, take a camel ride at sunset and enjoy a traditional dinner.

1 DAY TOUR TO CHEFCHAOUEN

Discover the typical Moroccan food with a local guide.

PROPOSED ITINERARY

8:00/KASBAH: Start your day in Tangier by visiting the kasbah, and the museums of the Kasbah and Ibn Batutta.

11:00/MEDINA: Tour the medina of the city and do some shopping.

12:00/ LUNCH: Refuel at one of the restaurants traditional buildings in the historic center.

16:00/CORNICHE: Get to know the city's promenade.

18:00/CAFÉ HAFA: The restaurant/ café with the best views of Tangier. The best time to go is at sunset.

20:00/DINNER: End the day in style at a restaurant overlooking the sea or medina. The 'Morocco Club' restaurant is a great option.

1 DAY TOUR TO CHEFCHAOUEN

Visit the city of Tangier with a private local guide.

TOURS

FREE TOURS

Lodging in Tangier

BEST AREAS OF TANGIER

1 MEDINA
This is the most authentic experience, staying in the alleys of the medina among the locals, restaurants, and stores.

2 CORNICHE
Stay in a hotel along the promenade overlooking the sea. The Corniche is very close to the medina.

3 KASBAH
It is located at the highest point of the city, in a central part near the medina. It has a multitude of restaurants and cafés.

4 ACHAKAR
Area far from the center. Its advantage is that it is close to the airport and beaches. Therefore, it is a quieter area than the other options above.

Riads/Dars

DAR TANJA BOUTIQUE HOTEL

Boutique hotel close to Tangier's golf course in a quieter environment. It has its own restaurant.

HOTELS TANGIER

📍 Dar Tanja, Villa Charrat

DAR NOUR

It is located in the historical center of Tangier. Traditionally decorated and with a bar on its fantastic terrace.

📍 20, Rue Gourna

🛏 Lodging: Tangier

Inexpensive (<$30)

DAR GARA

Hotel located in the kasbah of Tangier, near the medina. The hotel has equipped kitchen and terrace with views of the city.

📍 51 Rue Zaitouni

BAYT ALICE HOSTEL

Hostel located in the medina near restaurants and stores. In its terrace, it is easy to meet other travelers.

📍 26 Rue Khatib

Mid Range ($30-80)

RIAD AMR

Nice riad located in the kasbah, near the medina. It has a terrace and restaurant and all rooms have private bathrooms.

📍 Rue Lokous

KASBA WHITE

Lodging in the kasbah of Tangier, near the tourist points. The rooms are comfortable and air-conditioned.

📍 Rue El Gourna

Luxury (>$80)

PAL AIS ZAHIA HOTEL & SPA

Elegant riad located in the kasbah. All rooms have a living room and the hotel serves a delicious breakfast.

📍 Rue de la Marine N°76

THE MAISON OF TANGER

In the center of Tangier with a modern Moroccan style. It has a swimming pool, massage service and hammam.

📍 Rue Al Mabarra N°9

HERCULES CAVE

Food in Tangier

FOODS TO TRY

In Tangier, the specialty is seafood and fi sh, since the city is located in a very important port. I recommend you to try it:

1) Fish Tajines: especially anchovies and swordfish.

2) Fried squid.

3) Harira: a hearty Moroccan soup made of lentils, chickpeas and tomatoes.

🍽 Restaurants: Tangier

Saludable

ALMA KITCHEN & COFFEE

Excellent if you are looking for a healthy, delicious and different from traditional foos option. They serve delicious breakfasts and meals throughout the day. It is a 10 minute walk from the medina.

📍 Rue Antaki Place Des Nations

🕐 10:00am-11:30pm

MADE IN HEALTHY

This restaurant focuses on preparing delicious healthy meals. They have a wide variety of salads, poke bowls and delicious poached eggs. It is a 25 minute walk from the medina.

📍 Q5GR+CJC, Tangier

🕐 12pm-11:30 pm

🍽 Restaurants: Tangier

Breakfast / Coffee

CAFÉ À L'ANGL AISE

One of the most famous restaurants in Tangier. It is located located in the Kasbah and offers everything from coffee and tea, to Moroccan food and traditional breakfasts.

📍 37 Rue de la Kasbah

🕐 9am-10:15pm

LA TERRASSE - DAR EL KASBAH (KASBART)

Kasbart offers delicious sandwiches and natural juices. Although it is a restaurant that also offers Moroccan food and has a nice terrace.

📍 14 Rue de la Kasbah

🕐 10am-10pm, Tue-Sun

Lunch / Dinner

LE SAVOIR DE POISSON

Restaurant that does not have a menu, they only offer the fish of the day. For many travelers, it is the best fi sh they tasted on their trip to Morocco. Although the service is slow, every minute of waiting is worth it.

📍 Escalier Waller 2

🕐 1-5pm, 7:00-10:30pm

ABOU TAYSSIR - SYRIAN RESTAURANT

Fantastic Syrian restaurant where you can't leave without tasting their falafel. It has very reasonable prices and is located in the medina.

📍 11 Rue Italie Bab el Fahs

🕐 10am-12am

Traditional Moroccan

AHLEN RESTAURANT

One of the best rated traditional restaurants in the medina. They highlight their dishes of vegetarian tajine and grilled sardines. In addition, they have delicious homemade desserts.

📍 8 Rue des Postes

🕐 12-11PM, Thu, Tue

CHEZ HASSAN BAB KASBAH

Another travelers' favorite restaurants in Tangier. It is located near the Kasbah and has economic prices. In their menu they have fish and traditional grilled meats.

📍 8 Rue de la Kasbah

🕐 12:30-11:30pm

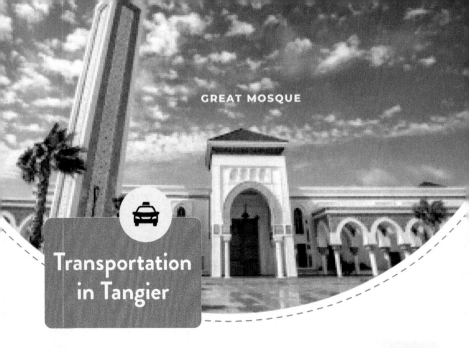

GREAT MOSQUE

Transportation in Tangier

 AIRPORT

<u>Minutes and km to the center:</u>
15 minutes/ 13 km.

- **Option 1:** cream-colored cabs from the airport. It usually costs $25-30.
- **Option 2:** ask your hotel to send you a trustworthy cab with a fixed and agreed price.
- **Option 3:** to avoid stress, you can book a cab transfer from this link.

TRANSPORTATION IN TANGIER

- **Walk:** the city is small. In 30 minutes you can get everywhere.
- **Cabs:** agree on the price or pay attention to whether the taximeter is on. There are no cab apps.

Transportation from
CHEFCHAOUEN

BUS | 2.5 H | $5
Recommended option
www.ctm.ma

CAB | 2 HOURS | $40

Transportation from
RABAT

TRAIN | 1.25 H | $8
Recommended option
www.oncf.ma

BUS | 4 HOURS | $7
www.ctm.ma

Chefchaouen

Medina | Blue village

↑ Here you will find

RECOMMENDED DAYS
1-2

Chefchaouen, or Chaouen for short, is also known as the "blue pearl". This is because the town center, houses and streets are painted in shades of blue.

I recommend that you spend 1 or 2 days leisurely strolling through the handicraft stalls and streets of this beautiful town.In addition, its beauty is enhanced by being in the midst of the Rif Mountains.

INSTAGRAM

CHEFCHAOUEN
DE @1HOURTRAVELGUIDES

What to do:
Chefchouen

1 WALKS THROUGH ITS BLUE ALLEYS

Walking the narrow blue streets of Chefchaouen is quite a spectacle. Tourists take the opportunity to take photos in every corner of the town.

Although there are several theories as to why Chefchaoen is blue, the most popular dates back to the time of the Holy Inquisition. Sephardim who were expelled from Spain, painted the streets and houses blue since it is the color of the sky, to remember the existence of God.

2 SUNRISE/SUNSET

One of the most popular activities in Chefchaoen is to watch the sunrise and sunset from one of its natural viewpoints or from the top of your hotel.

3 SPANISH MOSQUE

It is a mosque built around 1920 during a period of the war.

You can get there by walking about 30 minutes up a hill. It is a great place to watch the sunset.

4 GO TO RESTAURANTS WITH A VIEW

For excellent views of the blue village, I recommend that you go to one of its restaurants with a terrace.

Some of the most popular ones are Chez Aladdin, Bab Ssour and Cafe O'clock.

5 PLAZA UTA EL-HAMMAM

The most charming square in town. Sit in one of the restaurants or cafés to contemplate the local life.

Tours

CHEFCHAOUEN FROM FEZ

Visit the most important tourist attractions with a local guide.

HAMMAM

Experience one of the most authentic activities: a Moroccan spa.

CHEFCHAOUEN FROM TANGIER

Visit the city from Tangier on a day trip.

PRIVATE TOUR IN CHEFCHAOUEN

Explore the blue village with a local guide.

PROPOSED ITINERARY

7:00/PHOTOS: if taking pictures is your thing, I advise you to get up early to take pictures before it is flooded with tourists.

9:00/PLAZA OUTA EL HAMMAM: visit the most beautiful square of Chefchaouen and stop for breakfast or tea.

16:00/MEDINA: visit the handicraft stalls of Chefchaouen and purchase traditional items.

19:00/SUNSET: walk to the Spanish Mosque for some spectacular views of Chefchaouen.

20:30/DINNER: end the day with dinner on a terrace with a view.

TOURS

FREE TOURS

Lodging in Chefchaouen

BEST AREAS

1 **MEDINA**

Most travelers choose to stay in the medina of Chefchaouen. This is where most of the hotels, restaurants and craft stores are located. Although during the day the streets are crowded with people, at night it is a quiet area because there is little nightlife in this town.

2 **OUTSIDE THE MEDINA**

Some travelers prefer quieter areas, without so many tourists and even in the nature. The advantage of staying outside the medina is that the accommodations are easier to find, since they are not located in a labyrinth of alleys.

Riads/Dars

LINA RYAD & SPA

Located in the heart of Chefchaouen, the accommodation features an indoor swimming pool, hot tub and spa.

HOTELS

 Rue Moulay Hassan I, Mdaqa

DAR JASMINE

The accommodation is 1 km from the center, which has a beautiful outdoor area with garden, swimming pool and city views.

 Av. Ras Elma

🛏 Lodging: Chefchouen

Inexpensive (<$30)

AMINA HOUSE

Hotel located in the medina, decorated in white and blue tones. It offers mountain views from the terrace.

📍 Quartier Souika, Dreb Chebli ° 6

RIAD SAKURA

One of the favorite hotels of travelers in Chefchaouen. It is located next to the medina and has great views.

📍 Av Sidi Abdelhamis Q/msalla

Mid Range ($30-80)

DAR HANNAN

Traditional Moroccan hotel with a modern touch. All rooms have a living room and private bathroom.

📍 Rue Kiklana, Bab Souk 11

DAR SABABA

Excellent value for its moderate price. It has a traditional style and has fantastic views of the village.

📍 Rue Kaiklana N4 Quartier Souk

Luxury (>$80)

DAR ECHCHAOUEN MAISON D'HÔTES & RIAD

Spectacular accommodation with swimming pool, garden and the best views of the city and mountains.

📍 Route Ras El Ma, Quartier El Onsar

RIAD NILA

Elegant hotel of Moroccan decoration with a modern touch, which has its own hammam. Centrally located.

📍 Rue El Haj El Mokhtar Quart

Food in Tangier

Breakfast / Coffee

CAFÉ CLOCK RESTAURANT

The most famous dish of this restaurant is the camel burgers. They mix international and Moroccan dishes. Perfect place to stop by for breakfast.

📍 22 Rue Youssef El Fassi

🕐 9:30am - 9:00pm (Tue-Sun).

BILMOS

One of the best restaurants in Chefchaouen. They have vegetarian and vegan options of traditional dishes. They have a very friendly friendly and affordable prices.

📍 Place Outa El Hammam

🕐 8am-11:59pm

ALADDIN RESTAURANT

Restaurant decorated in traditional Moroccan style. It is located in one of the most famous squares of Chefchaouen and has very affordable prices for traditional dishes.

📍 17 Rue Targi, Place Outa Hamam

🕐 7am-11:45pm

PIZZERIA MANDAL A

If you want a break from traditional Moroccan food, stop by this pizzeria. One of the few places in Morocco to eat good pasta and pizza.

📍 Avenue Hassan II Angulo Sebanin

🕐 12pm-2:00am

Lunch / Dinner

Traditional Moroccan

CAFE RESTAURANT SOFIA

Cozy traditional restaurant located in the heart of Chefchaouen. It has delicious and cheap food. They also have vegetarian and vegan dishes.

📍 Place Outa Hammam

🕐 12:15pm-10:30pm, Tue-Sun

BELDI BAB SSOUR

Restaurant well known in Chefchaouen for its delicious traditional meals and vegetarian options. They serve meals at noon and in the evening. It is located in the medina of the blue village.

📍 No 5 Rue El Kharrazin

🕐 12:00-10:30 pm, Tue-Sun

 Transportation in Chefchaouen

✈ AIRPORT

Chefchaouen has no airport. The closest ones are those of Tangier (128 km) and Tetouan (67 km).

TRANSPORTATION IN CHEFCHAOUEN

- **Walk:** it is a small town where you will be walking all the time through its narrow streets.
- **Cab:** just outside the medina you can find cabs to move around the city.
- **Grand cab:** if you prefer a cheaper cab to travel between cities, you have the option of taking a shared cab. The price is economical, but you have to wait for the taxi to fill up before it starts the ride.

Transportation from
TANGIER

BUS | 2.5 HOURS | $5
Recommended option
www.ctm.ma

CAB | 1.2 HOURS | $40

Transportation from
FES

BUS | 4.5 HOURS | $8
Recommended option
www.ctm.ma

CAB | 3.5 HOURS | $60

Fes

RECOMMENDED DAYS
2-3

Fez is declared a World Heritage City by UNESCO. It has the oldest and largest medina in northern Africa.

The most exciting thing about this destination is to walk through its labyrinth of alleys (it has more than 10,000). In them you will find hundreds of handicraft stalls of fabrics, spices and other traditional Moroccan products.

INSTAGRAM

FÈS
DE @1HOURTRAVELGUIDES

CHOUARA TANNERY

What to do:
Fes

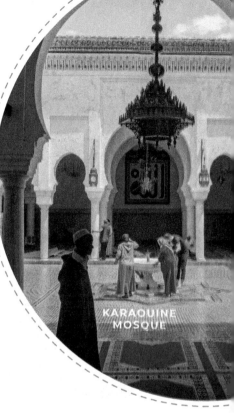

KARAOUINE MOSQUE

1 BOU INANIA MADRASA

One of the most architecturally beautiful buildings in Fes. It is a former school where the Koran was taught. Highlights for its elegant interior courtyard with beautiful geometric patterns.

Although there are two other famous Madrasas (El-Attarine and El-Cherratine) they cannot be visited by non-Muslims.

📍 3268+VW6, Rue Talaa Sghira

🕐 8am-6 pm, Tue-Sun

💲 $2

2 MEDINA

The historic center of Fes is the oldest (9th century) and largest in North Africa. The medina has more than 10,000 alleys, so you will have a hard time finding your accommodation or restaurants, even if you use GPS.

The charm of this place lies in walking around aimlessly enjoying the hundreds of handicraft stalls.

3 TANNERY

This is the place where the hides for leather products are colored and produced. The most famous tannery is the "Chouara Tannery". On your visit you will receive mint leaves, as the smell in the place is intense and very unpleasant. The visit is free of charge.

4 UNIVERSITY/ MOSQUE KARAOUINE

It is the oldest university in the world (which has never ceased to function). Although non-Muslims are not allowed to visit, you can appreciate the place from the terraces of the surrounding buildings.

5 JNAN SBIL GARDENS

If you want to escape from the hustle and bustle of the medina, visit this oasis of tranquility among flowers and palm trees.

📍 Avenue Moulay Hassan

🕐 During daylight

💲 Free

Things to do: Fes

6 DAR EL-BL ATHA MUSEUM
Museum with beautiful Andalusian-style architecture and gardens built in 1897. It houses traditional artifacts from the region, such as pottery, carpets and other textiles.

📍 Bab Guissa, Batha

🕐 9am-4pm, Wed-Mon

💲 $2

7 DAR EL-MAKHZEN
Palace for royal use, located in the new part of the medina (Fès El-Jedid). Although it cannot be visited, it is worth to know the impressive gateway to the palace.

8 MERINID TUMBS
They are located on a hill in the southern part of the outskirts of the city. From there you have a spectacular view of the medina. There are the tombs of the royal Merinid family, a Berber dynasty that ruled between the 13th-15th centuries. You can get there by cab and a short walk.

9 SOUKS
These are the main souks or markets to visit in the medina:
1) Chouara Tannery: leather.
2) Seffarine Square: metal.
3) Attarine Street: spices and herbs.
4) Nejjarine Square: wood.
5) Rcif Market: fresh produce.
6) Henna Souk: henna and cosmetics.
7) Zaouia Moulay Idriss II Souk: textiles and religious articles.

10 MEDINA GATES
These are the most famous access gates of the medina:
1) Bab Bou Jeloud (Blue Porch).
2) Bab Rcif (northwest of the medina).
3) Bab Ftouh (south of the medina).

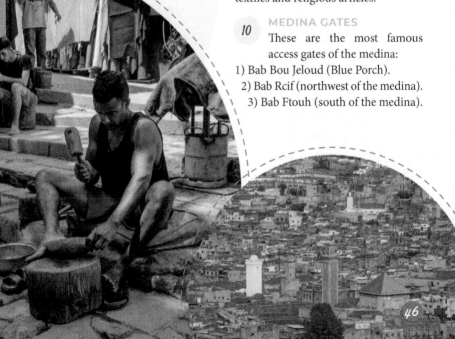

Tours in Fes

GUIDED TOUR IN THE MEDINA

Discover the secrets of the medina of Fes with a local guide.

TRADITIONAL HAMMAM

Visit a luxurious hammam to receive a massage and Moroccan beauty treatments.

TOUR TO THE SAHARA FROM FES

Do not leave Morocco without visiting the Sahara Desert.

MEKNES/VOLUBILIS TOUR

Visit the Roman city of Volubilis and the imperial city of Meknes.

PROPOSED ITINERARY

↓

8:00/BOU INANIA MADRASA: time to start your day in Fes at this building of beautiful architecture.

9:00/MEDINA: Lose yourself in the alleys of the largest medina in Morocco. Shop for handicrafts in the various souks.

12:00/MEAL: stop for lunch in a restaurant in the medina to be close to your next stop.

13:30/CHOUARA TANNERY: visit the place where leather products are made and where you can take one of the most famous photos of Fes.

16:00/COOKING LESSON/ HAMMAM: end the day with one of these 2 traditional Moroccan activities.

TOURS

FREE TOURS

DAR EL-MAKHZEN

Lodging in Fes

BEST AREAS

1 MEDINA

The most authentic area of Fes. Here you will find most of the traditional riads among 10,000 alleys. It can be difficult to find your accommodation even if you have the exact address.

2 VILLA NOUVELLE

The modern area of Fes. It is located 10 minutes by cab from the medina.

3 BATHA

The Batha area is located near the Jnan Sbil Gardens and next to the medina. It is a less intimidating area than the medina since the accommodations are easier to find, but it is still close to the historic center.

Riads/Dars

RIAD LAAROUSSA

Located in a 17th century palace in the medina. It has a beautiful terrace from where you can see the medina.

HOTELS

📍 3, Derb Bechara

RIAD SEMLALIA

Riad located in the medina with terrace, garden and outdoor pool. The staff will make you feel at home.

📍 20, Derb Sornass Ziat

🛏 Lodging: Fes

Inexpensive (<$30)

MEDINA SOCIAL CLUB

Good opportunity to stay in a beautiful riad at low cost. It is located in the medina and has a large terrace.

📍 11 derb el menia el wosta, talaa kebira

RIAD FEZ UNIQUE

Moroccan style lodging located in the heart of the medina. It has a terrace, restaurant and shuttle service from the airport.

📍 Derb Ben Salem

Mid Range ($30-80)

HOTEL & SPA DAR BENSOUDA

Traditional style hotel in the medina of Fes. It has an Arab bath where beauty treatments and massages are offered.

📍 N°14 Zkak El Bghel, Quettanine

RIAD AL MAKAN

Beautiful traditional Moroccan style hotel. It stands out for its beautiful inner courtyard and very friendly staff.

📍 8 Derb El Guebbas, Batha Medina

Luxury (>$80)

RIAD RCIF & SPA ORIGINALE

Wonderful riad located in the medina of Fes. The personal service is exquisite and the breakfast on the terrace is memorable.

📍 Avenue Ben Mohamed El Alaoui El Onsar

RIAD FEZ NASS ZMANE

An architectural jewel in the heart of Fes. It has very comfortable beds and terrace with views.

📍 16 Derb Bennis Douh

Food in Fes

FOODS TO TRY

1) <u>Pastille Fes style:</u> it usually has pigeon meat wrapped in layers and covered with powdered sugar and cinnamon.

2) <u>Mechoui:</u> slow cooked roast lamb. It is usually served with Moroccan bread (khobz) and a mixture of salt and cumin.

3) <u>Tajin:</u> this dish is simmered in a clay pot and is prepared with preserved lemons and olives in some of the restaurants in Fes.

🍽 Restaurants: Fes

Healthy

BISTROT DE SAVEURS

Located in Ville Nouvelle, outside the medina, in this restaurant you can choose your salad from more than 40 ingredients. Sandwiches, pasta and seafood options are also available.

📍 13 Avenue Ahmed Chaouki

🕐 11:30am-10pm

VEGGIE PAUSE

This restaurant focuses on preparing delicious healthy meals. They have a wide variety of salads, poke bowls and delicious poached eggs. It is a 25-minute walk from the medina.

📍 Q5GR+CJC, Tangier

🕐 12pm-11:30 pm (Mon-Sun)

🍽 Restaurants: Fes

Breakfast / Coffee

CAFÉ CLOCK

Popular café offering a wide variety of breakfast, lunch and dinner dishes. Café Clock is very popular in Morocco since it is based in Marrakech, Chefchaouen and Fes.

📍 7 Derb el Magana

🕐 9am-11pm

CINEMA CAFÉ

Charming café located near the entrance of the medina. It offers delicious healthy and western breakfasts with a Moroccan touch. Good prices and indoor, street, and an outdoor terrace.

📍 8 Sidi Lkhayat

🕐 8am-11pm

OLD MILL RESTAURANT AND CAFÉ

One of the best known restaurants, located next to one of the entrance gates of the medina. It combines dishes from the Mediterranean and Moroccan.

📍 Blue Gate, Fez

🕐 12:30-11 pm

GRILL ADE ADIL

This restaurant is part of a chain, although the menus are different in them. This restaurant, located in the historical part, specializes in khobz sandwiches. Its main ingredient is grilled meat.

📍 Rue Mohammed El Hansali

🕐 12-9pm

Lunch / Dinner

Traditional Moroccan

LA MORILLE

One of my favorite restaurants in Fes. It is located in the Ville Nouvelle area and has a modern look. Its highlight is the special menu, which includes 4 Moroccan salads, tajine and choice of dessert or drink.

📍 17 Ave Allal Ben Abdellah

🕐 12pm-12am

THE RUINED GARDEN

This small but cozy café offers avocado toast, cake, tea and coffee on its menu. It is very close to the sea and most of its seats are on the street, so it is perfect to observe the daily life.

📍 5 Rue Abdelaziz Al Fachtali

🕐 10am - 7pm (Tue-Sun).

Transportation in Fes

 AIRPORT

<u>Minutes and km to the center:</u>
18 minutes/ 13 km.

- **Option 1:** at the airport there are official cabs with fixed prices.
- **Option 2:** public bus. It is the cheapest option (about $3) and takes about 45 minutes. Take the bus line 16.
- **Option 3:** to avoid stress, you can book the cab transfer from this link.

TRANSPORTATION IN FES

- **Walking:** especially in the medina, where no vehicles are allowed.
- **Cabs:** cabs will try to say that the fare is $5. But try to negotiate as rides are usually much cheaper.

Transportation from
CHEFCHAOUEN

BUS | 4.5 HOURS | $8
Recommended option
www.ctm.ma

CAB | 1.2 HOURS | $40

Transportation from
RABAT

BUS | 2 HOURS | $5
Recommended option
www.ctm.ma

TRAIN | 3 HOURS | $6
www.oncf.ma

Meknes

RECOMMENDED DAYS
1-2

Meknes is a city just 40 minutes by train from Fes. It stands out for being one of the 4 imperial cities (ancient capitals) of Morocco.

In this destination you can find places with a lot of history and architecturally important buldings:

- Moulay Ismail Mausoleum
- Madrasa Bou Inania
- Roman city of Volubilis
- Sacred city of Moulay Idriss

Volubilis

Historic buildings

↑ Here you will find

BOU INAIA MADRASA

What to do:
Meknes

1 MEDINA

Stroll through the alleys of the medina to get a glimpse of the local life of Meknes. Although it is not as large as the medinas of Fes or Marrakech, it also has a great charm.

2 MOULAY IDRISS MAUSOLEUM

One of the most beautiful buildings in Morocco that you can visit. The building has a great historical and spiritual importance. The mausoleum is dedicated to Moulay Idriss II, descendant of the Prophet Mohammed.

📍 Rue Sarag

🕐 9am-6:30pm

💲 $2

3 BOU INANIA MEDRASA

Former Koranic school of the 14th century. Its inner courtyard with a fountain, geometric patterns and tiled floor will take your breath away. Unlike other buildings, this one can be visited.

📍 Rue des Souks en Sebbat

🕐 8am-12pm; 3pm-6pm

💲 $1

4 EL-HEDIM SQUARE

El-Hedim Square is the liveliest part of the city. It is located next to the door of the eighteenth century Bab Mansour. Local people

EL-HEDIM SQUARE

gather there at sunset and you can find plenty of restaurants.

5 VOLUBILIS

Ancient Roman city, founded in the third century B.C. It is located just 30 minutes drive from Meknes. Due to its good state of preservation and historical importance, it is considered a World Heritage Site by UNESCO.

📍 31 km northwest of Meknes

🕐 8am-1 hour before sunset

💲 $7

6 MOUL AY IDRISS (CITY)

One of the sacred cities in Morocco. Here is the tomb of Moulay Idriss I. It is only 5 km from Volubilis. Noted for being on top of a hill and its houses painted white.

VOLUBILIS

Tours in Meknes

TOUR FROM FES

One day tour to visit Meknes, Volubilis and Moulay Idriss from Fes.

TOUR FROM RABAT

Day tour to visit Meknes, Volubilis and Moulay Idriss from Rabat.

TOURS

FREE TOURS

PROPOSED ITINERARY

↓

8:00/HISTORIC CENTER: start the day getting to know the Porta Bab Mansour, El-Hedim Square and the Moulay Ismail Mausoleum.

11:00/MEDINA: walk through the medina, before stopping for lunch.

12:00/LUNCH: time to eat and recharge your batteries in a restaurant of the historic center.

13:00/VOLUBILIS: take a cab to the most important Roman City in Morocco.

15:30:00/MOULAY IDRISS: if you still have time and strength, stop by to know this sacred city.

19:00: end your intense day in Meknes with dinner at El-Hedim Square.

Lodging in Meknes

BEST AREAS

1 MEDINA

Many of the accommodations and restaurants are located in the alleys of the medina. Unlike the medinas of Fes and Marrakech, here you will not have much trouble finding your hotel as it is not as large or as complicated to navigate as the other medinas mentioned above.

2 EL-HEDIM SQUARE

It is located next to the medina and close to all the tourist attractions of the city.

3 VILLE NOUVELLE

The new part of the city, farther away from the tourist attractions and where more modern hotels are located.

Riads/Dars

RIAD LE PETIT KSAR

Beautiful riad with an unbeatable quality-price ratio. The rooms are comfortable and the staff very attentive.

HOTELS

📍 28 Rue Tiberbarine

RIAD YACOUT

Luxurious riad built in 1830. It has a beautiful inner courtyard with a fountain, and a terrace with solarium.

📍 22 Place Lalla Aouda

🛏 Lodging: Meknes

Inexpensive (<$30)

RYAD BAB BERDAINE

Cozy riad at a very good price, located in the medina of Meknes. The rooms are spacious and comfortable.

📍 7 Derb Moussa

RIAD DAR ZIDANE

Quiet accommodation, 7 minutes drive from the medina. The treatment of the hosts is exquisite.

📍 15 Rue Arrazi - Quartier Saada

Mid Range ($30-80)

RIAD ROYAL

This riad is so well preserved and decorated in the traditional style, that it will make you feel like you are sleeping in a museum.

📍 14, Rue Ain El Anboub Hammam Jdid

RIAD RITAJ

Riad with very beautiful rooms decorated in a traditional way. It is located in the heart of Meknes, next to the El-Hedim Square.

📍 13, Sidi Amer Bouaouada

Luxury (>$80)

DAR MEKNES TRESOR

Riad located in the center of the city. It stands out for having a breakfast and a swimming pool where you can relax.

📍 3 Derb Himich Hay Touta El Onsar

HOTEL BELLE VUE MEKNES

Recently built modern hotel located on the outskirts of the city. The hotel is perfect if you are looking for a quieter area.

📍 Rue Bnou Zouber, Ville Nouvelle

VOLUBILIS

Meals in Meknes

Lunch / Dinner

IL PANZEROT TO

Good Italian restaurants are hard to find in Morocco. Il Panzerotto is one of the few that has delicious pizzas. The owners pamper the business and the pizzas, since they are of Italian origin.

📍 5, Rue Abdelaziz Al Fachtali

🕐 11:30am-9:30pm, Mon-Sat

GILI KITCHEN MEKNES

Healthy food restaurant. If you are tired of traditional Moroccan food, here you can eat sandwiches, bowls and healthy breakfasts. It also has a wide variety of juices and coffee.

📍 Immeuble B1, Résidence Moulay

🕐 9am-11pm

Traditional Moroccan

RESTAURANT DAR BARAKA

A restaurant located in a traditional Moroccan dar. The owner of the restaurant serves you personally in a charming way. The establishment offers classic Moroccan dishes.

📍 5 Db My Abdallah Ahd Suezzara

🕐 12pm-11pm

AISHA

A traditional restaurant offering delicious Moroccan dishes in a cozy atmosphere. It is located in the labyrinth of alleys of the medina of Meknes.

📍 Koubat Souk Kababine

🕐 12pm-12am

MOULAY IDRISS

Transportation in Meknes

 AIRPORT

Meknes has no airport. The nearest is Fez, about 67 km away.

- **Option 1:** arrive in Fes by cab or bus and take the train to Meknes.
- **Option 2:** take a cab directly to Meknes (50 minutes, $30).

TRANSPORTATION IN MEKNES

- **Walk:** the city is small and you can go to most places in as little as a few minutes. only 30 minutes on foot.
- **Cabs:** be sure to agree on the price before getting in or pay attention to whether the meter is on. In Meknes, there are no cab apps, but you can find many on the street.

Transportation from
FES

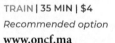

TRAIN | 35 MIN | $4
Recommended option
www.oncf.ma

BUS | 45 MIN | $3
www.ctm.ma

Transportation
MEKNES-VOLUBILIS

CAB | 30 MIN | $15
Recommended option

TOUR | 30 MIN | $25

Desert

 RECOMMENDED DAYS
2-4

In Morocco, you can't miss a trip to the Sahara Desert. It is about the size of the USA, 9.4 million km-squares in surfacce area!

Among the most interesting activities of this adventure are sleeping in a tent in a Berber camp, watching the infinite stars in a sky without light pollution, camel rides through the dunes at sunset and dancing with locals with a campfire at night.

INSTAGRAM

MERZOUGHA
DE @1HOURTRAVELGUIDES

What to do:
Sahara

1 CAMEL RIDE

The camel ride is usually included in the price of the tours. It is the first activity you do when you arrive at the Sahara Camp.

It is one of the most beautiful experiences, since it is usually done during sunset.

2 MUSIC AND DANCES WITH BERBER

After the traditional dinner, musicians from the Berber village gather with the tourists at the campfire. There, traditional songs are sung and played while dancing.

3 STARRY SKY

After the dances and songs around the campfire, there are still time to contemplate the stars. It is spectacular, since there is hardly any light pollution.

4 RISSANI

Only about 40 km from the Erg Chebbi dunes, you can visit this authentic Berber village.

This village was the first capital of the Aluí dynasty, which nowadays governs Morocco.

In addition, in Rissani you can find one of the oldest markets in Morocco, which was important in the trans-Saharan trade route.

5 STOPS DURING THE TOUR

Halfway to the Sahara, you can make several stops in the Draa Valley, Atlas landscapes, walled cities such as Aït-Ben-Haddou or Ouarzazate, and many other places of interest.

Experiences in the desert

In this section I will tell you about the different experiences you can choose in the desert area.

There are 3 places chosen by travelers:
- Merzouga (Sahara).
- Zagora (pre-Sahara).
- Agafay (Agafay desert).

It is also important to know that travelers can choose to live this experience on tour or on their own.

WITH TOUR
To choose the right tour location in the Sahara that suit your needs, you must take into account:
- Price / Distance from Marrakech.
- Dunes / Lodging.

WITHOUT A TOUR
It is important to know that there is no public transportation to go on your own. Therefore, car rental is essential. The average rental is $24, but you can rent cars from $6.

Hotels: on online hotel reservation platforms and Airbnb you can rent a night in these destinations, starting at$15.

Therefore, the experience can be a lot cheaper, although it requires a lot more planning.

TOURS IN THE SAHARA	MERZOUGA	ZAGORA	AGAFAY
Price	$100-300	$50-150	$30-100
Dunes	Erg Chebbi Dunes, the largest in the country.	Small dunes compared to those of Merzouga.	Rocky and desert terrain, but no dunes.
Distance from Marrakech	Farthest: 11 hours from Marrakech.	6 hours from Marrakech.	Nearest: 30 min-1 hour from Marrakech.
Lodging	Variety of options: from traditional Berber campsites to luxurious accommodations.	The less commercial experience: more rustic and less luxurious.	Variety: from glampings, to luxury and more basic accommodations.
Tour days	2-3 day tours	2-day tours.	Half or full day tours.

🚗 **Stops on** your trip to the desert

When you take a tour or drive to the Sahara desert in Merzouga, you will come across many points where it is worth your while to stop. Here is the list of places I recommend you to visit departing from Fes and Marrakech.

FES-MERZOUGA

- Ifrane: known as the "Switzerland of Morocco", this town is famous for its European-style architecture and beautiful parks.

- Azrou: in this destination you can find a great cedar park. But the highlight is to find a species of monkey called "barbershop".

- Midelt: a village located in the Atlas Mountains, in which you have panoramic views.

- Ziz Valley: a picturesque valley with thousands of palm trees, villages and views of the Ziz River.

MARRAKECH-MERZOUGA

- Tizi n'Tichka mountain pass: the most famous mountain pass in Morocco. It has stunning views of the valley.

- Aït-Ben-Haddou: one of the must-see places in Morocco on your trip. It has been declared a World Heritage Site by UNESCO.

- Ouarzazate: this village is perfect if you want to have lunch or stop to sleep on your long trip to the desert of Merzouga. There you can also visit the Atlas film studios.

- Skoura Oasis: famous for its palm tree plantations and Kasbah Amer-hildil.

- Valley of the Roses: known for its rose plantations and selling related products.

- Dades and Todra Gorges: these are 2 canyons between rock formations and rivers in the Atlas Mountains. The walls between the narrow roads, can reach up to 300 meters high.

- Rissani: historic city with a famous market and home to the Mausoleum of the historical figure Moulay Ali Cherif, ancestor of the current King Mohammed VI.

Desert Tours

SAHARA FROM MARRAKECH

Take a 3-day tour departing from Marrakech and camping in the dunes of Erg Chebbi in Merzouga.

SAHARA FROM FES

Take a 3 day tour departing from Fes and camp in the dunes of Erg Chebbi in Merzouga.

AGAFAY DESERT TOUR

Half day tour in the Agafay desert with traditional dinner.

DESERT TOUR IN ZAGORA

2 days tour to Zagora desert from Marrakech.

TOURS

FREE TOURS

PROPOSED ITINERARY

5:30/ SUNRISE: contemplate the first light of the day over the dunes of the Erg Chebbi desert.

9:00/CAMEL RIDE: one of the activities you can't miss in the desert.

10:30/KHAMLIA VILLAGE: visit this village, known for its Gnawa culture and music.

13:30/QUAD: Do you dare to cross the huge dunes of the desert on a quad biking and sandboarding?

19:00/DINNER: traditional dinner with green tea and music with Berber natives and dances around the bonfire.

21:30/STARS: contemplate the starry sky over the dunes.

Lodging in Merzouga

BEST AREAS

1 ERG CHEBBI DUNES

The most unique experience to stay in the Sahara. They are located near the village of Merzouga and you can reach them by camel or on a 4x4 (the trip can be organized by the hotel).

2 HASSI LABIED

Village close to Merzouga and the dunes. Quiet environment.

Here you can find simple accommodations or boutique hotels.

3 MERZOUGA

The closest village to the Erg Chebbi Dunes. If you are intimidated by the desert or want a more comfortable experience, here you have a wide variety of hotels. In Merzouga, you can also find stores and restaurants.

Riads/Dars

RIAD MADU

Luxurious riad in the village of Merzouga. Here you will have a comfortable experience and stay close to the desert dunes.

HOTELS

📍 Village Hassi Labied

RIAD MERZOUGA DUNES

Beautiful riad in an excellent location in Merzouga, close to the desert dunes.

📍 Ksar Tabomiat

🛏 Lodging: Merzouga

SAHARA WELLNESS CAMP

Camp among the desert dunes. The beds are very comfortable and the even have good wifi if you need connection.

📍 Lhou Ouargaga, Ksar Takoujte

DUNE MERZOUGA CAMP

Traditional desert camp. The staff will make sure that have a great experience.

📍 Ksar Hassi Labied

Middle Range

RIAD SUERTE LOCA MERZOUGA

Hotel with rooms decorated in Moroccan style. It has a swimming pool and patio to relax.

📍 Ksar merzouga

DESERT BERBER FIRE-CAMP

Beautiful Berber camp in the middle of the desert where you will be able to see the starry night sky.

📍 Merzouga

Luxury

LUXURIOUS MERZOUGA DESERT CAMPS

Luxurious Berber camp between the desert dunes. The hotel organizes transfers in 4x4 cars.

📍 Ksar Merzouga

SUNRISE SAHARA CAMP

Accommodation in modern capsules between the desert dunes. Arrival in camel to the camp.

📍 Hassilabied, 52202 Merzouga

Transportation in Merzouga

 AIRPORT

Errachidia (ERH) is the closest airport to Merzouga and the Sahara desert. It is located 55 km from Merzouga.

It has only domestic flights to Casablanca and Rabat and international flights to Paris.

In any case, in certain seasons there are no planes departing from this airport.

TRANSPORTATION IN MERZOUGA

- **Walking:** only recommended to go to the restaurants and stores in the village of Merzouga.
- **Cabs:** in Merzouga there are cabs that can take you to different nearby locations.
- **Hotel:** the hotels should arrange transfers to the desert camp on 4x4 cars or by camel ride.

Transportation from
FES

 BUS | 10 HOURS | $13
Recommended option
supratours.ma

 CAR RENTAL
7.5 HOURS

Transportation from
MARRAKECH

 TOUR | 10 HOURS
Recommended option

 CAR RENTAL
10 HOURS

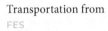

Ouarzazate

RECOMMENDED DAYS
1-2

It has become very popular for filming movies and series. "Gladiator" and "Game of Thrones" were filmed here.

The places to visit in Ouarzazate are not concentrated in the city, but in the surrounding area. On the way, you can find oasis, walled cities made of mud, film studios, valleys and breathtaking landscapes of the Atlas Mountains. Therefore you need a car rental or a tour to get to know this destination.

INSTAGRAM

OUARZAZATE
DE @1HOURTRAVELGUIDES

What to do:
Ouarzazate

1 AÏT-BEN-HADDOU

This fortress made of mud and adobe, has become one of the icons of Morocco. Movies and series have been filmed there, such as "Gladiator" and "Game of Thrones".

It is located about 30 km from Ouarzazate (30-45 minutes).

📍 30 km northwest of Ouarzazate

🕐 All day

💲 Free

2 TAOURIRT KASBAH

The only historic building in the city of Ouarzazate (the rest are in the surrounding area). The kasbah, built in the 18th century, is very well preserved.

3 ATLAS FILM STUDIOS

Morocco is the perfect place for film shooting because of its desert landscapes and low prices. In the Atlas Studios, numerous films and series have been recorded.

📍 N9 road (6km from Ouarzazate).

🕐 8am-6:30pm

💲 $6

4 TELOUET KASBAH

An architectural jewel made of mud and adobe. It has been partialy restored, so a part is still in ruins. This place was the former residence of the Glaoui family.

It is located about 40 km from Ouarzazate (1 hour drive).

5 SKOURA

Skoura is a village located only one hour away from Ouarzazate.

Its great attraction is the kasbah called Ameridil. It is a mud and adobe fortress in the middle of an oasis. The city is surrounded by palm trees, date palms and green fields.

In addition, Skoura also has a classic Moroccan market.

6 KASBAHS

The Ouarzazate area has other important mud and adobe fortresses in the towns of Tamnougalt, Tamegroute, Zagora and Oulad Othmane.

AÏT-BEN-HADDOU

Tours in Ouarzazate

OUARZAZATE AND SAHARA TOUR

Visit the main attractions of Ouarzazate on the way to the desert.

AÏT-BEN-HADDOU BY QUAD BIKE

Drive a quad to the most famous kasbah in Morocco, departing from Ouarzazate.

OUARZAZATE AND ZAGORA TOUR

Visit the main attractions of Ouarzazate on your way to the Zagora desert.

1 DAY TOUR FROM MARRAKECH

Day trip to Aït-ben-Haddou and Atlas studies from Marrakech.

PROPOSED ITINERARY

↓

8:30/KASBAH TAOURIRT: start the day by touring the kasbah located next to Ouarzazate.

9:30/ATLAS FILM STUDIOS: take a guided tour of Morocco's most famous film studios.

11:30/AÏT-BEN-HADDOU: finally get to know the most famous kasbah of Morocco.

13:30/MEAL: time for lunch at a restaurant near the kasbah.

15:30/PALMERAIE: take a walk in the oasis and the palm grove that is is located next to Ouarzazate.

19:00: end the day with dinner in a traditional restaurant of Ouarzazate.

TOURS

FREE TOURS

Lodging in Ouarzazate

ATLAS STUDIOS

BEST AREAS

1 MOHAMED V AVENUE
The main avenue that crosses the city. There you can find a multitude of hotels, restaurants and stores.

2 KASBAH TAOURIRT AND HISTORICAL CENTER
Very close to Mohammed V Avenue, but in a traditional zone between alleys.

3 ATLAS FILM STUDIOS
Just a few minutes away from Ouarzazate, you will find the studios of cinema. Some hotels are located in this area.

4 AÏT-BEN-HADDOU
In the surroundings of the most famous kasbah in Morocco, you can find various accommodations.

Kasbahs/Riads

DAR CHAMAA
Located in the palm grove of Ouarzazate, overlooking the Atlas. It has a large garden with swimming pool and a dreamlike architecture.

HOTELS

KASBAH TAMSNA
If you want to stay in a traditional kasbah, this is a great option. It is located next to the Atlas Studios.

📍 Tajda Bp 701 Tarmigte

📍 Hay Tamassinte

🛏 Lodging: Ouarzazate

Economic

AFGO HOSTEL

Simple hostel located in Ouarzazate. Good place to meet travelers in its common areas. It has a terrace with views.

📍 Avenue el Ouaha Tarmigt Ouarzazate

BIVOUAC LOT OF STARS

Lodging in the middle of nature in a quiet environment. The rooms are beautiful, traditional style tents.

📍 Palmeraie Tajda Cr.Tarmigte

Middle Range

RIAD DAR BERGUI

Hotel decorated in Moroccan style that resembles a kasbah. It is located 800 meters from the center, so it is in a quiet place.

📍 Sidi Hssain

HÔTEL RIAD DAR DAÏF

It is one of the most popular hotels in the area. A beautiful kasbah where you can sleep for an affordable price.

📍 Douar Talmasla

Luxury

LE PETIT RIAD MAISON D'HÔTES

Luxurious accommodation in Berber style. It has a beautiful patio and swimming pool. It is located near down-town and the airport.

📍 Avenue Moulay Abdellah

RIAD TAMA & SPA

A beautiful hotel with traditional architecture, but with rooms modern. It has a garden, swimming pool and solarium.

📍 Hay Tamassinte

Ouarzazate Restaurants

ACCORD MAJEUR

Restaurant with a very friendly service and exceptional quality. The cuisines are French and Italian and you can even take wine glasses. Undoubtedly one of the best restaurants in the area.

📍 Av Mansour Eddahbi

🕐 7-10pm

THE FULL SUN

One of the best restaurants in Ouarzazate where they have dishes with a good value for money. They serve traditional dishes Moroccan and international.

📍 N° 706 Avenue Moulay Rachid

🕐 7am-11:45pm

Lunch / Dinner

THE KASBAH DES SABLES

The hotel is located in a kasbah in Ouarzazate. It is traditionally decorated and serves typical Moroccan food. It is a bit difficult to find, but it is worth having lunch or dinner here.

📍 195 Hay Aït Gdif

🕐 12-3pm, 7-11:59pm; Mon-Sat.

LA TERRRASSE DES DELICES

Totally recommended the visit to this restaurant, although it is a little far from Ouarzazate. It is located in a beautiful hotel in the middle of an oasis. You can eat on a terrace with pool and great views.

📍 Azeouane Rachid Douar Fint Taharbile

Typical Moroccan

Transportation in Ouarzazate

AÏT-BEN-HADDOU

 AIRPORT

<u>Minutes and km to the center:</u>
10 minutes/ 2 km.

- **Option 1:** The airport is located next to the city. It costs between $2-5.
- **Option 2:** ask your hotel to send you a trustworthy cab already with the agreed price.
- **Option 3:** to avoid stress, you can book a cab transfer from this link.

TRANSPORTATION IN OUARZAZATE

- Walk: the city is small. Walk to go to the restaurants and stores.
- Cabs: be sure to agree on the price before getting in or pay attention to whether the meter is on. In Ouarzazate, there are no cab apps.

Transportation from
MARRAKECH

BUS | 5 HOURS | $7
Recommended option
www.oncf.ma

CAR RENTAL
4 HOURS

Transportation from
MERZOUGA

CAR RENTAL
6 HOURS

TOUR | 7 HOURS

Marrakech

RECOMMENDED DAYS
2-4

Visiting Marrakech is a sensory experience. It is a city with a great mix of colors, sounds, smells and stimuli for the senses.

Marrakech is a more touristic city with many places of interest to visit. There you can visit beautiful gardens, museums and buildings of worship.

It is also a good point of connection if you want to visit the coast, the Atlas Mountains or the desert.

INSTAGRAM

MARRAKECH
DE @1HOURTRAVELGUIDES

What to do:
Marrakech

1 MEDINA
One of the most important and chaotic medinas in the country. Hundreds of craft stalls are concentrated there. Beware of motorcycles, pickpockets and swindlers.

2 JEMAA EL-FNA SQUARE
The most authentic square in Morocco. The square is a spectacle when the sun begins to set: you will see musicians, snake charmers, street food stalls and all kinds of shows.

3 JEWISH QUARTER (MELLAH)
In this enclave you will find narrow alleyways, synagogues and Jewish community merchants.

4 KOUTOUBIA MOSQUE
Impossible not to see this mosque with an imposing minaret 70 meters high. It is the largest mosque in Morocco, which can accommodate up to 20,000 people. Only Muslims can enter the mosque.

5 MARRAKECH MUSEUM
The museum is housed in a traditional Moorish style 19th-century palace. It houses a collection of contemporary art and historical artifacts.

📍 Ben Youssef Square

🕐 9am-6:30pm

💲 $7

6 JARDIN MAJORELLE/ YVES SAINT LAURENT'S MUSEUM
The garden and museum are located in the same complex. You can buy individual or joint tickets.

-Jardin Majorelle: known for its exotic plants and vibrant blue walls. It was designed by painter Jacques Majorelle in the 1920s.

-YSL Museum: it is related to the designer Yves Saint Laurent. It talks about his work, legacy and fashion.

📍 Yacoub El-Mansour Av.

🕐 9am-6pm

💲 $7-10

BEN YOUSSEF MADRASA

LE JARDIN SECRET

7 BAHIA PALACE

One of the icons of Marrakech. It is a palace with extensive patios, ornate halls and large gardens.

📍 Riad Zitoun El Jedid

🕐 9am-4:30pm

💲 $7

8 RAHBA KEDIMA SQUARE

One of the most important squares of Marrakech. It is located in the medina of the city, with craft stalls and near the Ben Youssef madrassa.

9 BEN YOUSSEF MADRASA

Founded in the 14th century, it is one of the most important and beautiful buildings in Morocco. Students from all over the world came here to study the Koran.

📍 Kaat Benahid

🕐 9am-6pm

💲 $7

10 LE JARDIN SECRET

Another wonderful garden with plants brought from all over the world. The building and garden were restored after being abandoned for many years.

The building houses photography, art and history exhibits. Also has a good coffee shop called "Café Sahrij".

📍 121 Rue Moussaine

🕐 9:30am-6:30pm

💲 $7

11 TANNERIES

Although not as extensive and spectacular as those in Fez, Marrakech is also home to tanneries where leather products are made.

You can find them south of Bab Debagh Street. Although they are hidden from view, their intense smell will indicate that you have arrived. Don't forget to take some mint to help curb your nausea.

12 SOUKS

These are the main souks and handicraft products in the medina:

- Souk Semmarine (clothing and textiles).
- Souk Rahba Kedima (spices).
- Souk Attarine (oils and perfumes).
- Souk Haddadine (metal products).
- Souk El Bahja (ceramics).
- Souk El Kessabine (leather).
- Souk des Bijoutiers (jewelry).
- Souk El Koutoubia (books).
- Souk El Koutoubia (libros).

Tours

QUAD AND CAMEL RIDE

A very complete tour with a quad ride through the desert, a camel ride and visits to Berber villages.

COOKING CLASS

Learn how to cook traditional dishes with a local family.

OZOUD WATERFALLS

Visit the Ozoud Waterfalls from Marrakech. Includes boat ride.

TOUR OF THE HISTORIC CENTER

Visit with a local guide the medina of Marrakech and the Bahia Palace.

PROPOSED ITINERARY

↓

9:00/JARDIN MAJORELLE: start your day at this iconic garden and YVES museum.

10:30/BAHIA PALLACE: visit another must-see place in Marrakech.

12:00/MEAL: time to recharge your batteries in a local restaurant. medina.

13:30/MEDINA: walk through the various souks of the medina and shop for traditional products.

15:30/BEN YOUSSEF MADRASA: do not miss this beautiful school.

19:00/JEMAA EL-FNA SQUARE: experience the madness of the square an the sunset, and eat at its street stalls.

TOURS

FREE TOURS AGADIR

JEMAA EL-FNA

Lodging in Marrakech

BEST AREAS

1 MEDINA
This is the heart of the city and where the majority of the city's hotels, restaurants and stores are.

2 GUELIZ
Modern district of Marrakech with wide avenues, fashionable stores and trendy restaurants. It is about 10 minutes by cab of the medina.

3 HIVERNAGE
Area of luxurious hotels, spas and nightclubs. It is located next to Gueliz only about 10 minutes by cab from the center.

4 PALMERAIE
North of Marrakech, between palm groves and nature. It is a quiet area in luxury resorts.

Riads/Dars

RIAD DAR MARRAKCHA

One of the most aesthetic riads in Marrakech. The hotel staff will make you feel at home.

HOTELS

📍 18 Derb Ben Allal, Medina

RIAD MELHOUN & SPA

The facilities, location, staff treatment, and rooms are excellent in this riad.

📍 99 Derb Sidi moussa La Bahia

🛏 **Lodging:** Marrakech

Economic

BE NOMAD

Hostal located in the alleys of the medina, very close to the main attractions. It has a very friendly staff.

📍 Rue Bensaleh, Derb Bouanane N°37

THE CENTRAL HOUSE

Riad converted into a beautiful guesthouse with a terrace overlooking the Atlas. It has a swimming pool in its inner courtyard.

📍 Amssafah 32, Quartier Assouel

Middle Range

RIAD VIS TA VIE

Hotel in the heart of Marrakech. It has a very attentive staff, delicious breakfast and shuttle service from the airport.

📍 N° 6 Derb Ben Allal, Ben Saleh

RIAD ALIA

Riad decorated in a traditional way but with modern rooms. It is located in the Jewish quarter, very close to the tourist attractions.

📍 Derb Manchoura 38, Mellah

Lujo

RIAD SOFYAN & SPA

Beautiful riad located near the tourist attractions. It has massages, spa and hammam services.

📍 25 Derb Slima, Medina

RIAD AL LOUNE

Luxurious riad located in the medina. It has a terrace with sun loungers on the roof. Also massage service and a hammam.

📍 77, Derb El Cadi, Azbezt, Medina

Food in Marrakech

1) Eggplant Zaalouk: a delicious eggplant salad served cold and mixed with tomato, garlic and spices.

2) Camel, lamb or rabbit tajine: traditional Moroccan dish but served with camel, lamb or rabbit meat.

3) Couscous: although some restaurants only serve it on Fridays, it is one of the most popular dishes in Marrakech.

🍽 Restaurants: Marrakech

Healthy

MAZEL CAFE

It is located in Tinsmiths Square, just 5 minutes walk from the Bahia Palace. Although it does not present itself as a healthy restaurant, it has very tasty and healthy bowls and sandwiches.

📍 8 Place des Ferblontiers

🕐 10am-8:30pm

MANDALA SOCIETY

If you prefer a break from traditional Moroccan food and eat healthy, I recommend this restaurant. It has specialty coffee and a great variety of salads, quesadillas, bowls and healthy food.

📍 159 Rue Riad Zitoun el Jdid

🕐 9:30am-10:30pm

🍽️ Restaurants: Marrakech

Breakfast / Coffee

CAFÉ DES ÉPICES

Located in the medina with a terrace with great views. Although they also serve lunch and dinner, the restaurant stands out for its traditional Moroccan breakfast: omelet, fruit salad and breads.

📍 75 Derb Rahba Lakdima

🕐 9am-11pm

BACHA COFFE HOUSE

This place is worth a visit if only to see the Bacha Palace while sipping tea/coffee. They have a selection of more than 200 varieties of coffee and dishes that combine Moroccan cuisine and French.

📍 Dar el Bacha, Rte Sidi Abdelaziz

🕐 10am-6pm

Lunch / Dinner

NOMAD

One of the most popular restaurants in the medina. It offers a more elaborate traditional cuisine and elegantly designed inside. Book in advance to eat on the terrace.

📍 1 Derb Aarjane

🕐 12-10:30pm

LE KILIM

One of the best restaurants I visited in the Gueliz area. They serve from breakfast to lunch and dinner. On their menu, they offer Moroccan food, grilled fish and healthy and vegetarian options.

📍 N° 3 Rez-de-Chaussée

🕐 9am-1am

Typical Moroccan

CHEF LAMINE HADI MUSTAPHA

It stands out for the lamb roasted slowly on a grill under the floor. In addition, they offer the rest of traditional Moroccan dishes. They have one location in the medina and another in Gueliz.

📍 Derb Semmarine

🕐 10am-1am

FINE MAMA

Located very close to the Jemaa el-Fna Square. It offers a large selection of traditional dishes, mezze, sandwiches and Moroccan pastries. They have a cozy interior and a terrace with good views.

📍 89 Pass. Prince Moulay Rachid

🕐 9:30am-12am

🍸 Nightlife: Marrakech

Bars/Cocktails

THE BARS, ROYAL MANSOUR MARRAKECH

Although you might not have thought of drinking alcohol in Morocco, it is worth having a cocktail at this bar/restaurant for a different experience.

📍 Rue Abou Abbas El Sebti

🕐 11am-10pm

THE PERGOLA

If you prefer to have a few drinks while you relax on a terrace, this is the perfect place. They also have restaurant service and sometimes, they have live music.

📍 7/8 Derb Chaabane - Riad Zitoun

🕐 11am-11pm

BAROMÈTRE MARRAKECH

Modern and elegant restaurant/bar. Although the prices are high, it is worth having a drink at this bar if your budget allows it. The place has an ambiance with loud music.

📍 Rue Moulay Ali Guéliz Residence

🕐 6pm-1am, Mon-Sat

LE CHURCHILL BAR

Luxurious bar that has creative (and very expensive) drinks. It has a modern decor with traditional touches. It is located inside the hotel where Winston Churchill stayed.

📍 Avenue Bab Jdid

🕐 6-11pm

Bars/Cocktails

Nightclubs

KABANA

Terrace where you can dine, have cocktails and even dance with DJs at the end of the night. The decoration and the menu have modern and international styles, but with Moroccan touches.

📍 Derb Semmarine

🕐 10am-1am

THEATRO

The best nightclub in Marrakech and one of the few places in Morocco where you can dance until late. They have performances of dancers and acrobats every weekend.

📍 Rue Ibrahim El Mazini Es Saadi

🕐 11:30pm-5am

BAHIA PALACE

Transportation in Marrakech

✈ AIRPORT

<u>Minutes and km to the center:</u>
21 minutes/ 5 km.

- **Option 1:** blue cabs from the airport ($15). Prices are fixed and usually do not put the taximeter on.
- **Option 2:** ask your hotel to send you a reliable cab.
- **Option 3:** to avoid stress, you can book with this link.

TRANSPORTATION IN MARRAKECH

- **Walk:** especially if you are going to visit the medina, as cabs are not allowed.
- **Cabs:** cabs in the medina charge a fixed tourist price of $5. But if you insist and ask, some cabs agree to lower the price to $2-3. You can also use the apps "Careem" and "InDrive".

Transportation from
ESSAOUIRA

BUS | 3 HOURS | $6
Recommended option
www.ctm.ma

VAN
2.25 HOURS | $25

Transportation
CASABLANCA

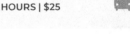

TRAIN | 2.75 HOURS | $6
Recommended option
www.oncf.ma

BUS | 3.25 HOURS | $6
www.ctm.ma

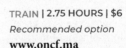

Taghazout

RECOMMENDED DAYS
1-2

Surf | Beaches

↑ Here you will find

Taghazout is a coastal town in the southwest of Morocco, known for its relaxed atmosphere, sandy beaches and unbeatable conditions for surfing.

This destination has a bohemian character and is not yet crowded with tourists despite its rapid growth in the last decade. It is located next to Tamraght, another former fishing village. Both villages have been reconverted to tourism through surfing, yoga, ealthy food, and other activities and beaches.

What to do:
Taghazout

1 SURF

Taghazout has become world famous for having perfect surfing beaches. Just 7 km away is Tamraght, another small fishing village where hundreds of travelers come to surf. The best surf schools are:

- Berbere Surf.
- Minth Surf.
- Surf School Morocco (Tamraght).

2 BEACHES

Whether for surfing or sunbathing, Taghazout has kilometers of sandy beaches where you can play sports or relax.

The best beaches in the area are:

- Taghazout beach.
- Imourane beach.
- Aghroud Beach.

3 AGADIR

Agadir is one of the most popular destinations for domestic tourists. The city was devastated in 1960 by a major earthquake.

It is only a 30-minute drive from Taghazout and features for its sandy beaches and surfing.

4 YOGA

Taghazout is a place that attracts health tourism. In addition to surfing, there are many people who do yoga. I recommend "Paradis Plage Surf&Spa", "Kalananda Yoga Studio" and "Om Yoga Taghazout Bay".

5 PARADISE VALLEY

About 50 km from Taghazout (1.5 hours by car or cab), you can go hiking in the Atlas Mountains. There you will find spectacular landscapes among palm trees, mountains and where you can refresh yourself in natural pools of crystal clear water.

6 SUNSET

Taghazout has spectacular spots to watch the sunset while watching surfers in action. I especially recommend the "Anchor Point" and the "Munga Guest House" and "Panorama restaurant".

Tours

TRADITIONAL COOKING CLASS

Learn how to cook typical Moroccan dishes with a local chef.

QUAD IN DESERT

Drive a quad bike in the desert dunes passing by traditional villages.

SWIMS IN LAKES BETWEEN MOUNTAINS

Travel to the Atlas Mountains where you can swim in lakes between beautiful valleys.

PROPOSED ITINERARY

↓

9:00/SURF: Start the morning with a surf lesson.

12:30/MEAL: recover energy at the restaurant "WOW".

13:30/TAGHAZOUT: time to stroll around and get to know the charming village of Taghazout.

14:30/ANCHOR POINT: get to this spot for incredible views of the sea and surfers in action.

16:00/BEACH: time to relax on the main beach of Taghazout.

19:00/DINNER: end your day in Taghazout in a restaurant with a view. (and alcoholic beverages if you feel like it) such as "La Favella".

SURFING CLASS

Learn to surf with a local instructor.

TOURS

FREE TOURS

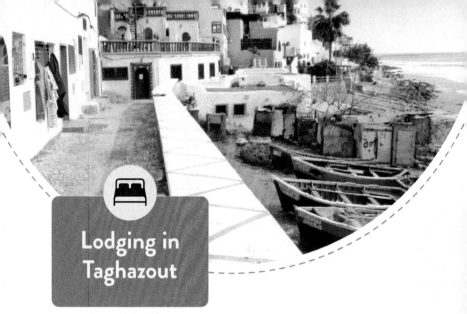

Lodging in Taghazout

BEST AREAS

1 **TAGHAZOUT VILLAGE**
The heart of the city and where most of the hotels, restaurants and travelers are located.

2 **TAGHAZOUT BEACHES**
You also have the option of staying in front of the sandy beaches of Taghazout.

3 **TAMRAGHT**
Surfing village located 10 minutes by cab from the center of Taghazout. It is smaller and quieter than Taghazout. It also has excellent beaches for surfing, places to eat healthy and practice yoga.

Coliving Space

NOMADICO

Coliving space in Tamraght where you can make friends from the moment you set foot in the house. It is a perfect space if you work remotely and want to be surrounded by a fabulous community of nomads. Or if you want to surf and are looking to meet other travelers.

 Tamraght

BOOK WITH THIS 5% DISCOUNT CODE

1HTRAVELGUIDES

🛏 Lodging: Taghazout

Economic

GOLVEN SURF

Hostel located just a few meters away from the sea. It has a nice terrace and all rooms have private bathroom.

HOTELS

AZOUL HOSTEL TAGHAZOUT

Budget hostel where you can easily meet other travelers. It is located just 4 minutes walk from the beach.

📍 Taghazout center

📍 Taghazout center

Middle Range

TAGHAZOUT HILL RETREAT

Very quiet hotel in an area only a few kilometers from Taghazout. It has a garden and an outdoor swimming pool.

📍 Ait Bihi Taghazout

SUNNY WAVE TAGHAZOUT SURF & YOGA

Hostel with a very attentive staff and good atmosphere among travelers. Located near the beach.

📍 Taghazout center

Luxury

HYATT PLACE TAGHAZOUT BAY

Luxurious hotel 3 kilometers from Taghazout. It has an outdoor swimming pool and traditional Moroccan massage service.

📍 Taghazout Bay Tourist Station

MUNGA GUESTHOUSE

One of the most beautiful hotels in Taghazout. It is located on the first line and has an infinity pool.

📍 Rue Iwlit TaghazoutMedina

Food in Taghazout

🍽 Restaurants: Taghazout

Healthy

LET'S BE HEALING FOOD

Perfect restaurant to eat healthy and to change a bit from the traditional food.
It is located in the village of Tamraght. They have delicious bowls, juices, smoothies and toasts.

📍 1 National Route, Tamraght

🕐 9am-11pm

OHANA POKÉ & VITAMIN BAR

Another great option in Tamraght to eat something healthy and tasty. They serve delicious poke bowls and hamburgers with fresh ingredients.

📍 Rue de la Jeunesse, Tamraght

🕐 12pm-10pm, Tue-Sun

🍽 Restaurants: Taghazout

Breakfast / Coffee

RED CLAY CAFÉ

Very good place to start the day with breakfast. You have a mix of Moroccan and international dishes and vegan options. The restaurant staff is very friendly and will make you feel at home.

📍 1 National Route, Taghazout

🕐 7:30am-5:00pm, Fri-Mar

LE HAPPY BELLY

This restaurant is also an organic products store. They serve breakfast, lunch and dinner made with healthy ingredients. The dishes they prepare are of international cuisine.

📍 Route Essaouira, Tamraght

🕐 9am-10pm

WORLD OF WAVES

Excellent restaurant where you can relax watching the waves of the sea and the sunset. They have a menu with traditional dishes, hamburgers and even serve alcoholic beverages.

📍 Font de mer Villa Tizniti

🕐 8am-10pm

RESTAURANT LE SPOT

Quiet place to go to eat with your friends. They have varied economic food, such as pizzas, burgers, and Moroccan food. Do not miss their mural with the great surfers who visited Le Spot.

📍 Taghazout Centre

🕐 8:30am-11pm

Lunch / Dinner

Traditional Moroccan

DAR JOSEPHINE

One of the best traditional restaurants in the area. They serve classic Moroccan dishes. Reservations are recommended as the restaurant is usually full.

📍 Centre Ville Taghazout centre

🕐 9am-11pm

LA FAVELLA

Elegant restaurant where you can find dishes of Moroccan cuisine. Although the restaurant has a modern touch, as you can drink alcoholic beverages and eat Italian-inspired dishes.

📍 17 Ilwite, Taghazout

🕐 4pm-11:30pm, Tue-Sun

Transportation in Taghazout

 AIRPORT

<u>Minutes and km to the center:</u>
the nearest airport is Agadir, 43 km from Taghazout (40 km from Agadir). minutes).

- **Option 1:** Taxis cost about $40.
- **Option 2:** ask your hotel to send you a trustworthy cab already with the agreed price.
- **Option 3:** to avoid stress, you can book the cab transfer from this link.

TRANSPORTATION IN TAZHAOUT

- **Walk:** the city is tiny, so you can walk to all the places you want to visit. You can even walk from Taghazout to Tamraght along the promenade.
- **Cabs:** Taxi apps do not work in Taghazout.

Since this destination does not have good connections, you should go to Agadir to take a cab or bus from there.

Transportation from
AGADIR

CAB | 30 MIN | $15   TAXI

Transportation from
Essaouira to AGADIR

BUS | 2.75 HOURS | $6
Recommended option
www.ctm.ma

CAR RENTAL
2.25 HOURS

Essaouira

RECOMMENDED DAYS
1-3

Medina | Surf

↑ **Here you will find**

Essaouira is a charming fishermen's town located on the Atlantic Ocean.

This destination will captivate you with its beautiful walled medina and and its cobbled streets. Houses are beautifully painted in shades of white and blue. The center of Essaouira is full of craft stalls and art galleries.

Moreover, Essaouira is a perfect place to get started in the practice of surfing. It has perfect beaches for sunbathing and sports.

INSTAGRAM

ESSAOUIRA
DE @1HOURTRAVELGUIDES

What to do:
Essaouira

1 MEDINA

The historic center of Essaouira is the main point of the city. It is formed by narrow alleys with houses and walls painted in white and blue.

There you can find most of the restaurants, hotels, food stalls and handicraft stores.

2 SURF

The beach next to the medina in Essaouira is perfect for surfing. I recommend surfing at this beach if you do not have a rented vehicle or if you are a beginner.

Surf schools are easily found there.

But if you prefer quieter beaches, I recommend "Sidi Kaouki", "Moulay Bouzerktoun" or "Sidi M'Barek". Although to reach these beaches you need your own vehicle.

3 PORT SQALA

The port, which is located next to the medina, is one of the most important areas of Essaouira, where fishermen and traders sell fish.

There you can contemplate a colorful fleet of ships, with hundreds of seagulls flying in the surroundings.

The architecture of the Sqala port, with its ancient ramparts and cannons, gives a historical touch to the experience.

4 MOUL AY HASSAN SQUARE

It is the heart of Essaouira. A square surrounded by white buildings and cafés with terraces.

It is a meeting area for local families and artistic groups where theatrical or musical performances.

It is especially recommended to go at sunset. This is the time when you will see the most bustle in the square.

5 EAT SEAFOOD

Essaouira is famous for its delicious seafood, sardines and good places to eat. Especially recommended are these restaurants: Chez Sam, Le Patio and Triskala Café Restaurant.

Tours in Essaouira

1 DAY TOUR FROM MARRAKECH

Visit the beach and the famous port of Essaouira with a stop at the argan oil cooperative.

SURF LESSON IN ESAUIRA

Learn how to surf with this 2-hour lesson at the main beach of Essaouira.

HORSEBACK RIDING ON THE BEACH

Horseback riding along the beaches of Essaouira with a stop for lunch.

ESAUIRA TOUR WITH GUIDE

Discover all the secrets of Essaouira with a local guide.

PROPOSED ITINERARY

↓

9:00/MEDINA: start the day touring this UNESCO World Heritage medina.

11:00/SKALA DE LA VILLE: discover the ramparts of Essaouira with a view of the Atlantic Ocean.

12:00/MEAL: the restaurants have fresh seafood just brought in. So take advantage of the opportunity!

13:30/BEACH: stroll, sunbathe or take a camel ride on the beach, which is located next to the medina.

16:00/PORT ESAUIRA: the fi shermen finish their day and it is a spectacle to stroll around the port and shop in the medina.

20:00/DINNER: dinner in a restaurant with terrace or sea view.

TOURS

FREE TOURS

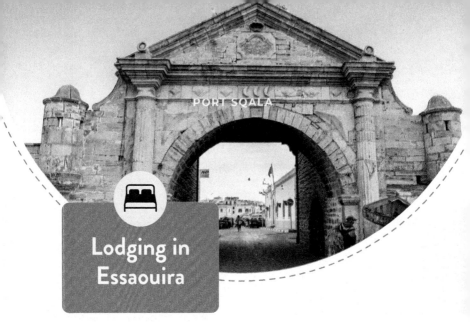

PORT SQALA

Lodging in Essaouira

BEST AREAS

1 MEDINA

The main area where most tourists choose to stay in Essaouira. It is the historic part, where most restaurants, craft stores and where there is more atmosphere in the city. Despite having narrow alleys, it is not as difficult to find your way around as in the medinas of Marrakech or Fez.

2 CORNICHE/BEACH

This area is located next to the medina. If you want a quieter area, with sea views and beach, I recommend this part of Essaouira. Walking, you can easily reach the historical part.

Riads/Dars

RIAD CHBANATE

Beautiful riad located next to the city walls. It has spacious rooms decorated in traditional Moroccan style.

HOTELS

📍 179, Chbanate

RIAD EMOTION

This luxurious and centrally located riad features a terrace with sun loungers, a garden with fountain and terrace overlooking the city.

📍 18, Rue Malek Ben El Morahal

🛏 Lodging: Essaouira

Economic

RIAD LUNETOILE

Hotel overlooking the beach located in the medina. It has rooms with typical decoration and Moroccan lounge.

📍 191, Rue Sidi Mohamed Ben Abdullah

DAR HALIMA

Centrally located guesthouse with traditional decoration. It has a terrace with views and a very friendly staff.

📍 N 33 Rue Qadi Ayad

Middle Range

RIAD MELLAH

Lodging located in the medina with beautiful views to the sea. The beach is less than 1 km from the property.

📍 9 Rue Tafilalt, Mellah

VILLA GARANCE

Ecological Riad with Berber, Jewish and Arab influences. They offer a rich breakfast and its location is unbeatable.

📍 10, Rue A. Eddakhil

Luxury

RIAD KALIFA

Luxurious riad perfect for family stays or those looking for tranquility and sea views.

📍 Rue Yamen 4 Bis

RIAD ESPRITBLEU

Beautiful riad with modern decoration. Centrally located, very close to the beach. The terrace overlooks the sea.

📍 52 Rue d'Agadir, Ahl Agadir

Food in Essaouira

1) M'semen: square-shaped breads that are usually eaten at the breakfast. It is usually eaten in a simple, salty or sweet version (chocolate, honey or cheese).

2) Seafood: Essaouira has an important port next to the medina. Restaurants often are specialized or have delicious fresh fish dishes on their menu.

3) Amlou: similar to peanut butter, but even richer. It is made from peanut butter, honey and argan oil.

🍽 Restaurants: Essaouira

Healthy

MANDALA SOCIETY

The most famous health food restaurant in Essaouira. It offers in its menu delicious breakfast and lunch dishes. Highlights its 'Budha bowl' with vegetables, quinoa, hummus and argan oil.

📍 Istiqlal Ave.

🕐 9:30am -10:30pm

LE CORAIL

One of the best vegan options in Morocco. In its menu, it has a wide variety of juices, spring rolls, tajines and vegan burgers. It is located in the medina.

📍 BP423 Place Al Khaima

🕐 9am-10pm

🍽 Restaurants: Essaouira

Breakfast / Coffee

PICKNICK CAFE

Charming café with a careful design and menu focused on brunch dishes, healthy, specialty coffee, juices and smoothies. Their salmon bowls with avocado, and chicken with vegetables stand out.

📍 22 Rue Youssef El Fassi

🕐 9:30am - 9:00pm, Tue-Sun

CAFE L'ESPRIT

This small but cozy café offers avocado toast, tea cake and coffee on its menu. It is very close to the sea and most of its seating are on the street, so it is perfect to observe the daily life.

📍 N, 05 rue abdelaziz Al fachtali

🕐 10am - 7pm, Tue-Sun

SAFRAN CITRON RESTAURANT

Restaurant that offers a gastronomic experience close to the haute cuisine, but in a comfortable atmosphere. Located in the medina, it specializes in fish and traditional dishes.

📍 12 Rue Laalouj

🕐 11:30am-10:30pm

CHEZ ZAK

Small restaurant specializing in fish and seafood. Although it is not the cheapest, its highlight and most famous dish is the grilled lobster. Try to sit on the terrace if available.

📍 56 Rue Elkhabbazine

🕐 9am-10pm, Sat-Wed / 12-10:30pm, Thu-Fri

Lunch / Dinner

Typical Moroccan

VILLA DES HAUTS MOGADOR

Cozy restaurant located along with 12 other restaurants in the Chrib Atay square (in the middle of the medina). It has traditional dishes such as couscous. But his specialty is the grilled sardine and octopus tajine.

📍 Place Chrib Atay, Rue Laalouj

🕐 10am - 11pm (daily)

RESTAURANT BAGHDAD

Located in a not so touristy part of the medina, this restaurant specializes in cooking sardines, lobsters, traditional salads and tajines. The food is delicious and the prices are moderate.

📍 12 Rue d'Agadir

🕐 11am-11pm

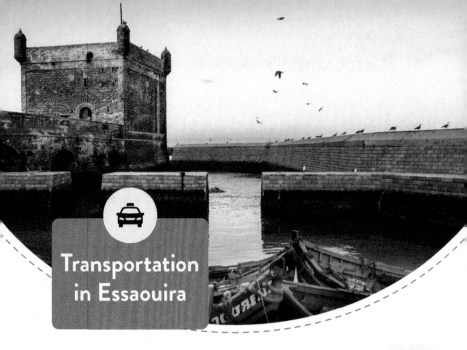

Transportation in Essaouira

 AIRPORT

<u>Minutes and km to the center:</u>
22 minutes/ 15 km.

- **Option 1:** blue cabs from the airport ($15-20). It is normal to pay this price without a taximeter.
- **Option 2:** ask your hotel to send you a trustworthy cab with the agreed price.
- **Option 3:** to avoid stress, you can book the cab transfer from this link.

TRANSPORTATION IN ESSAOUIRA

- **Walk:** the city is small so you can walk and get to know the city.
- **Cabs:** agree on the price and pay attention to the taximeter. In Essaouira, there are no cab apps.

Transportation
MARRAKECH-ESSAOUIRA

BUS | 3 HOURS | $6
Recommended option
www.ctm.ma

VAN
2.25 HOURS | $25

Transportation
CASABLANCA-ESSAOUIRA

BUS | 7 HOURS | $10
Recommended option
www.ctm.ma

PRIVATE TRANSPORTATION
4 HOURS | $30-40

Casablanca

 RECOMMENDED DAYS
1 DAY

Casablanca is the largest city in Morocco with 3.4 million inhabitants. It is also the economic capital of the country.

The city has a less traditional medina than the other cities I recommend. But it is worth a visit to this destination for its impressive mosque. The Hassan II mosque is the second largest mosque in Africa and the only one that non-Muslims in Morocco can visit.

Casablanca does not have so many historical tourist sites, but it is an interesting destination for its mix of architecture and is home to a great gastronomic diversity.

HASSAN II MOSQUE

What to do:
Casablanca

1 HASSAN II MOSQUE

The only mosque you can visit in Morocco. Built next to the sea in 1993, with an imposing minaret of 210 meters. It is the most touristic place in Casablanca.

📍 Sidi Mohammed Ben Abdallah Blvd.

🕐 9am-4pm

💲 $13

2 RICK'S CAFE

Establishment built in 2004, tribute to the movie "Casablanca". It is decorated as in the movie and is you can drink alcoholic beverages and eat Moroccan and international dishes.

3 CORNICHE

The corniche is a promenade where you can find restaurants, cafés and beaches. It is a safe point, where you can walk to get to know the city better.

4 MOHAMMED V SQUARE

This square is an iconic point of the city. It is located in the center and is surrounded by historical and administrative buildings.

There, neighbors usually gather to chat and stroll.

5 SKY 28

The Sky 28 bar is located on top of one of the 2 buildings called "Twin Towers".

At the bar, you can sip cocktails while enjoying panoramic city views from 115 meters.

6 MEDINA

One of the few old parts of Casablanca that has been preserved over time. In any case, it does not have color and traditional essence compared to that of Fez or Marrakech.

Tours

GUIDED TOUR IN CASABLANCA

Get to know the best tourist spots of the city with a private guide.

FOOD TOUR

Taste street food and the best Moroccan dishes with an expert guide.

GUIDED TOUR OF THE MOSQUE

Take a private tour of the Hassan II Mosque with a local guide.

PROPOSED ITINERARY

↓

8:00/HASSAN II MOSQUE: start the day in the most important tourist spot of Casablanca.

10:00/CORNICHE AIN DIAB: take a walk by the sea after leaving the mosque.

12:00/RICK'S CAFÉ: meet and eat at the famous café inspired by the Casablanca film.

14:00/MEDINA: : walk through the and alleys of the medina and reach the cathedral of Casablanca.

16:00/ARABIC LEAGUE PARK: observe the local life in this park surrounded by historic buildings and stop by to know the central market.

20:00/DINNER: dinner at La Sqala and a drink at the 'Sky 28 Bar'.

TRADITIONAL MOROCCAN SPA

Pamper your body and mind in a hammam, the traditional Moroccan spa.

TOURS   FREE TOURS

HASSAN II MOSQUE

Lodging in Casablanca

BEST AREAS

1 AIN DIAB

Area located next to the promenade and very close to the Hassan II Mosque. There is a multitude of hotels and restaurants.

2 SIDI BELYOUT

Area next to the United Nations park. Close to tourist attractions and the medina, but a little calmer.

3 MEDINA

The heart of the city. The accommodations are located between alleys in the old part of Casablanca. Here you can stay in boutique hotels and riads.

4 VILLA NOUVELLE

Urban center of Casablanca. It is an area with international hotels and close to restaurants, stores, restaurants, shops and modern attractions.

Riads/Dars

RIAD HAMDANI

Riad close to the airport and away from the hustle and bustle of the city. Its gardens and swimming pool are perfect for resting.

HOTELS

📍 Douar El Bouzanniene Nouacer BP 27 Deroua

RIAD TANJIL

Accommodation away from the chaos of Casablanca. Perfect to disconnect and spend a quiet stay.

📍 Awled saleh nouaceur Nouaceur

🛏 Lodging: Casablanca

LHOSTEL À CASABLANCA

Lodging located in a calm zone, 7 km away from the Hassan II mosque. The space has a garden and a terrace.

📍 6, Rue d'Aix Oasis, Maarif

HÔTEL ASTRID

Located in a central area with a good quality-price ratio. It has its own restaurant and spacious rooms.

📍 12, Rue 6 novembre, Sidi Belyout

Middle Range

RYAD 91

Comfortable, clean and in an unbeatable location: close to the medina, the train station and 2.5 km from the mosque.

📍 91, Rue de Fès, Dar-el-Beida

UNICO HOTEL

Modern hotel with Moroccan touches. It is surrounded by restaurants, stores and close to all points of tourism interest.

📍 5 Rue du Gabon, Sidi Belyout

Luxury

STAYHERE CASABLANCA GHAUTIER APARTMENTS

Modern and luxurious apartments located in a quiet area of Casablanca.

📍 Rue Hafi d Ibrahim, Sidi Belyout

ODYSSEE BOUTIQUE HOTEL CASABLANCA

Comfortable hotel where you will feel at home due to the friendliness of the staff. It is located in the center.

📍 Angle Rue Kamal Mohamed-Avenue

Food in Casablanca

FOODS TO TRY

1) Seafood or fish dishes, from fish and vegetable tajine to seafood pastilla.

2) Sardine skewers. In Casablanca they have an incomparable flavor since it is located next to the sea.

3) Harira with fish meatballs: thick and nutritious soup with fish meatballs.

4) Mechouia salad: fresh and spicy salad, which combines roasted peppers, tomatoes and onion with spices and olive oil.

🍽 Restaurants: Casablanca

Healthy

ORGANIC KITCHEN

One of the best and most famous healthy food restaurants in Casablanca. It offers a wide variety of vegetarian dishes, shawarmas, bowls, sandwiches and salads prepared with salmon or chicken.

📍 6-8 Rue Ahmed El Mokri

🕐 10am-10:30pm, Mon-Fri

NIYA

Vegan restaurant located in the Ghautier district. It is known for its creative vegan dishes. The restaurant is designed as an intimate space, as if it were a private living room or library.

📍 34 Rue Sebou

🕐 10am-9:30pm, Tue-Sat / 10am-5pm, Sun.

🍽 Restaurants: Casablanca

Breakfast / Coffee

KHOS

Restaurant that offers healthy breakfasts with ingredients such as quinoa, turkey, avocado, broccoli and arugula. Salads, juices and sandwiches are on the menu.

📍 44 Rue Annoussour

🕐 9am-5pm, Sun-Fri

HOLY BRUNCH

It is located in the trendy Gauthier district. It is known for its variety in the meals: from healthy options breakfast, such as food bowls, to indulgent options, such as tacos.

📍 Rue Al Bouhtouri

🕐 8am-7pm, Mon-Fri / 9:30am-7pm, Sat-Sun

Lunch / Dinner

CHEZ MICHEL ET HAFIDA

Excellent option if you are looking for fresh seafood at affordable prices. Located in the central market, it stands out for its dishes of grilled sardines and mussel stew accompanied by vegetables.

📍 Stall 192, Bd Mohammed V

🕐 10am-9:30pm, Tue-Sun

SOLAMO'S

Excellent choice for lunch aft er the visit to the Hassan II Mosque. It offers a varied menu of meals and breakfast, from traditional dishes, fi sh and healthy options.

📍 Bd d'El Hank

🕐 6am-12pm

Traditional Moroccan

THE SQALA

This restaurant is an institution in the city and is located in an 18th century fort. They prepare typical dishes and do not serve alcoholic beverages.

📍 Ibnou Hayane, 61 Rue jaber Bd d'Anfa

🕐 7am-11pm

SAVEURS DU PALAIS

One of the best traditional restaurants in Casablanca. Known for its varied Moroccan salads, kid tajine and traditional cakes.

📍 28 Rue Jalal Eddine Sayouti

🕐 10am-10:30pm

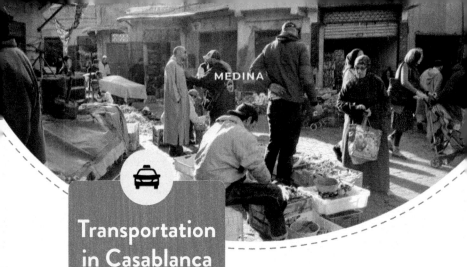

MEDINA

Transportation in Casablanca

AIRPORT

Minutes and km to the center:
40 minutes/ 36 km.

- **Option 1:** Taxis from the airport cost about $25-30.
- **Option 2:** there is a train from the airport to downtown (Casa Port Station): 45 min/$4.
- **Option 3:** to avoid stress, you can book a cab transfer from this link.

TRANSPORTATION IN CASABLANCA

- **Walk:** the tourist attractions can be visited by walking between them.
- **Cabs:** make sure you agree on the price before getting in the cab. Although there is no Uber, there are alternative apps: Careem, Roby, Heetch and Yassir. Apps don't always work, though.

STATIONS

- Bus station address: CTM Far (Rue Léon l'Africain).
- Train stations: Casa-Voyageurs and Casa-Port.

Transportation from
RABAT

TRAIN | 1 HOUR | $4
Recommended option
www.oncf.ma

BUS | 1.25 HOURS | $4
www.ctm.ma

Transportation from
ESSAOUIRA

BUS | 7 HOURS | $10
Recommended option
www.ctm.ma

PRIVATE TRANSPORTATION
4 HOURS | $30-40

Rabat

Medina | Kasbah

↑ Here you will find

☀ **RECOMMENDED DAYS**
1-2

Rabat, the capital of Morocco, perfectly combines modernity with historical heritage.

Located on the Atlantic coast, it has a traditional medina with handicraft stalls (less bustling than in other destinations).

You cannot miss a visit to the kasbah, with its cobblestone streets, ramparts and sea views.

A visit to the Mausoleum of Mohammed V and the Hassan Tower is also a must.

KASBAH

What to do:
Rabat

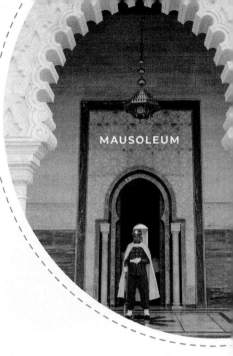

MAUSOLEUM

1 HASSAN TOWER AND MAUSOLEUM

Mausoleum built in honor of the late King Mohammed V.

It is located next to the Hassan Tower, which is part of a mosque that was never completed.

📍 Boulevard El-Alaouiyine

🕐 9am-6pm

💲 Free

2 KASBAH DOS OUDAIAS

This fortress with cobblestone streets and white-painted streets was built in the 12th century. It served as a refuge for the Moors expelled from Spain.

It has beautiful ocean views and is open 24 hours a day.

3 PORT

Next to the Kasbah, I recommend you to walk around the port area. In the afternoon/evening it gets crowded with locals strolling and eating at the promenade restaurants.

4 MEDINA

Rabat also has a medina with narrow streets where merchants sell handicrafts. It is a less chaotic medina than the ones in Marrakech and in Fez. Highlights include the Souk As Sebbat for spices and local products, the Souk es Sabbaghin for textiles and carpets, and the Souk Lghazel for jewelry and handicrafts.

5 CONTEMPORARY ART MUSEUM

Probably the best art museum in Morocco. Combines ancient, modern, Moroccan and international pieces of art.

📍 Moulay Hassan Av. & Allal Ben Av.

🕐 10am-6 pm, Wed-Mon

💲 $6

6 CHELLAH NECROPOLIS

Historical site with ruined buildings of Phoenician and Roman settlements. Some time later, it became a burial place under Islamic rule.

🕐 9am-6pm

💲 $7

Tours in Rabat

RABAT WALKING TOUR

Visit the most important tourist attractions with a local guide.

COOKING CLASS

Learn how to cook traditional dishes with a local family.

STREET FOOD TOUR

Discover the typical Moroccan food with a local guide.

TOUR FROM CASABLANCA

Get to know Rabat for a one-day trip from Casablanca.

TOURS

FREE TOURS

PROPOSED ITINERARY

↓

8:00/KASBAH: Explore the narrow streets of the fortification overlooking the Atlantic.

9:30/NECROPOLIS CHELLAH: time to visit the Roman ruins of Rabat.

12:00/MEDINA: walk through the medina, stalls of handicrafts and find a place to eat.

14:00/HASSAN II TOWER: visit the most famous tower of Rabat and the Mausoleum of Mohammed V.

16:00/ROYAL PALACE: walk along Mohammed V Avenue and see the Royal Palace from the outside.

20:00/DINNER: time for dinner at one of the restaurants on my list.

HASSAN TOWER

Lodging in Rabat

BEST AREAS

1 **MEDINA**
The heart of Rabat. A labyrinth of narrow alleys. You will find traditional accommodations, restaurants and stores. It is one of the oldest areas of the city.

2 **AGBAL**
Rabat's trendiest neighborhood with plenty of restaurants, stores and even some nightlife. 10 minutes by cab from the historic center.

3 **AV. MOHAMMED V**
Convenient for tourists who want to be close to the medina, but in an environment of stores and more modern restaurants.

4 **OCEAN**
Popular with tourists looking for a quiet area with sea views. It is only about 10 minutes by cab from the medina.

Riads/Dars

L'ALCAZAR
Elegant riad located near the medina and the sea. The rooms are spacious and traditionally decorated.

HOTELS

EUPHORIAD
Comfortable, beautiful and luxurious riad in the center of Rabat. The staff is very friendly and the terrace will amaze you.

📍 4 Impasse Benabdellah, Bab Laalou

📍 7-9 Impasse Kaïd Bargach

🛏 Lodging: Rabat

Economic

DAR RITA

Centrally located in the center of Rabat and near the beach. It has a large terrace where you can relax and get to know other travelers.

📍 22 Rue Lalla Oum Kenabech

DAR WASSIM EL GHALI

Budget hostel in the medina of Rabat. It is close to all tourist attractions and has a terrace with views of the sea.

📍 66 impasse Attara Rue des Consuls

Middle Range

RIAD DAR RABIAA

Very aesthetic accommodation with pastel green and white colors. It has a swimming pool in the inner courtyard. Located in the medina.

📍 Rue Hotel Chorfas 7

STAYHERE AGDAL ELEGANCE RETREAT

Modern and comfortable apartment-style accommodation. It is located in the district of Agdal, a more modern area of the city.

📍 76 Rue Oued Moulouya

Luxury

RIAD AMARIS

Centrally located and beautifully renovated riad. It has a terrace with a fountain and a furnished terrace.

📍 10, Avenue Lalla Hanou

DAR SHÂAN

Beautiful dar located in the heart of Rabat. The accommodation features a terrace with swimming pool and all rooms have a living room.

📍 Rue Jirari

MAUSOLEO

Lunch in Rabat

FOODS TO TRY

1) Fish skewers with chermoula sauce: Rabat offers excellent choices of fish and seafood, since it is by the sea.

2) Couscous with lamb: in Rabat it is served with tender lamb and fresh vegetables.

🍽 Restaurants: Rabat

Healthy

LA P'TITE EPICERIE DU TERROIR

Gourmet grocery store with 2 tables for dining. Delicious salads and sandwiches on the menu. The place has an Asian touch, since the chef used to live in Korea.

📍 7 Rue Benzart

🕐 10am-8pm, Mon-Sat

LA CASA DI CARTA

Italian-Moroccan restaurant that has healthy dishes on its menu, such as quinoa salad and grilled salmon. It offers pizza, pasta and Moroccan dishes, such as kebabs and rfissa on its menu.

📍 259F+CH8, Rue d'Oran

🕐 11am-11pm, Thu-Mon / 10am-11pm, Tue-Wed.

114

🍽 Restaurants: Rabat

Breakfast / Coffee

BOHO CAFE

Fantastic place for breakfast that mixes Moroccan and Western food. It is located near the Rabal Ville train station. Highlights include quinoa salad, sweet potato waffle, açaí bowls and coffee.

📍 10 Rue EL Yamama
🕐 9am-9pm, Tue-Sat
10am-9pm, Sun

LE MAITRES DU PAIN

This famous bakery in Rabat also works as a restaurant. You can choose from their meals, salads, meat skewers, sandwiches and hamburgers. The bread in this establishment is excellent.

📍 75 Av. Patrice Lumumba
🕐 7am-10pm

PIETRI PALACE

It is located in a square along other cafés and restaurants in the center of Rabat. Its menu includes food international, such as pizzas, pastas and sandwiches, or traditional Moroccan dishes.

📍 Rue Moulay Idriss al Akbar
🕐 7am-11:30pm, Mon-Wed 8am-11:30pm, Th-Thu-Fri 8am-12am, Sat 7am-12am

TIDE

Elegant Moroccan-European fusion restaurant specializing in seafood. One of its most outstanding dishes is grilled salmon with lobster sauce, accompanied by vegetables and mussels.

📍 9 Rue AL Mariniyine
🕐 12-3pm, 7-10pm, Tue-Fri 1-4pm, 7:30-11pm, Sat 1-5pm, Sun

Lunch / Dinner

Traditional Moroccan

DAR NAJI

Restaurant located next to the medina. It has a terrace from where you can see the walls of the medina. It has a wide range of traditional Moroccan dishes such as kebabs, couscous and tajine.

📍 Jazirat Al Arabe Av.
🕐 12-10pm

GIVING THE MEDINA

Hidden jewel in the medina of Rabat which also has a cooking school. The restaurant has a large variety of Moroccan dishes such as tajine, couscous and traditional Moroccan starters.

📍 3 Rue Benjelloul Souk Sebbat
🕐 12-4pm, 7-10pm, Tue-Sun (closed Mondays)

Transportation in Rabat

 AIRPORT

<u>Minutes and km to the center:</u>
20 minutes/ 11 km.

- **Option 1:** Airport cabs usually charge between $15-20.
- **Option 2:** bus to downtown with Alsa Bus. It costs $4.
- **Option 3:** to avoid stress, you can book a cab transfer from this link.

TRANSPORTATION IN RABAT

- **Walk:** you can reach all the tourist attractions on foot.
- **Cabs:** make sure you agree on the price before getting into the cab. There are also apps to order cabs online such as Carreem or Roby.

*The main station to take the train is called "Rabat Ville". It is the closest to the center.

Transportation from
CASABLANCA

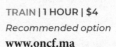

TRAIN | 1 HOUR | $4
Recommended option
www.oncf.ma

BUS | 1.25 HOURS | $4
www.ctm.ma

Transportation from
TANGIER

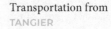

TRAIN | 1.25 HOURS | $8
Recommended option
www.oncf.ma

BUS | 4 HOURS | $6
www.ctm.ma

Safety in Morocco

Safety in Morocco

Is Morocco a safe country for tourism? My answer is YES, but with a few caveats.

In fact, it is one of the safest countries in Africa and the Middle East. Here are some risks and tips.

Risks

1. The risk of robbery with violence is very low.

2. But there is theft in places with large crowds, such as markets or squares. Normally, these happen without you realize.

3. Robbery is also possible with a tug on your backpack/bag from a motorcycle.

4. The risk of terrorism is currently low: the last attacks happened in Marrakech in 2011 and Atlas in 2018.

5. There is a risk of natural disasters, especially flooding during the rainy season (November to March) and earthquakes: Morocco is located in a seismic zone and many houses are not prepared to withstand large earthquakes.

6. Avoid remote areas of the Rif, Atlas and the border with Algeria and Western Sahara.

2. Markets and scammers

Markets

Especially in the markets of Marrakech and Fes, the vendors can be rude and even try to persuade you to buy their products agressively. What should you be aware when shopping in markets and not end up angry or frustrated?

- <u>Negotiate:</u> Be aware that in Morocco's markets you have to negotiate. It's part of the fun.

- <u>Never accept the first price:</u> you can lower it by more than half.

- <u>Tip:</u> to estimate the price, ask the price of the same item in different stalls.

- <u>Don't get angry:</u> and walk away if the seller gets angry.

Scammers

- You can find them in the medinas, squares or markets.

- They usually stop you with a "Hey buddy, where are you from?" or a "Do you need help?"

- As it is complicated to move in the labyrinth of alleys of the medinas (even Google Maps does not work). well there), the scammers try to take you "for free".

- They usually mislead you by saying that the street you are going to is closed. They will guide you for "free" to then ask you for a tip with an aggressive tone.

- Avoid locals who, without asking, want to show you the city or tell you the history of the place. They will always ask for money even if they initially say it is "free".

- These "friendly locals" may take you to a friend's craft stores where they will charge you a huge amount of money (then they make a commission).

- There are reports of scams where people try to befriend you, only to rob you 1-2 days later.

3. Women's *safety*

Although Morocco is a relatively safe country, women traveling alone or with a female friend report that it is a very uncomfortable experience:

- There are men who may make you uncomfortable with comments or whistles.
- There are reports of women being cornered in the alleys of medinas.

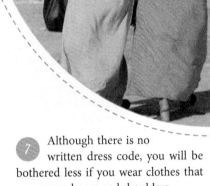

Tips

1. Go in company: women reduce harassment with company (especially from men).

2. Organized trips and tours are usually safer.

3. Be careful in markets, alleys and when walking at night.

4. With headphones and/or sunglasses, men will bother you less oft en.

5. Saying you're married or wearing a wedding ring usually works too (even if it's not true).

6. Learn to feel comfortable ignoring their comments and saying NO in Arabic ("La").

7. Although there is no written dress code, you will be bothered less if you wear clothes that cover your knees and shoulders.

8. It is not mandatory to wear a hijab (headscarf). But if you do not have brown hair, you will receive less attention when wearing a hat, cap or hijab.

9. Consider purchasing this safety item: "She's Birdie".

She's Birdie

4. **Other**
important data

1 LGTBI+

Although Morocco is one of the most open Muslim countries in terms of LGTBI+ rights, you have to keep in mind that homosexuality is forbidden. It is even punishable by imprisonment.

Please note:

- Beware of dating apps, as there are reports of police creating fake profiles.
- Beware of public displays of affection.
- If you are traveling with your partner, you will have no problem sleeping in the same room.

2 ALCOHOL

Alcohol consumption is legal in Morocco. But keep in mind:

- It is only sold in restaurants, hotels, bars and some supermarkets.
- Its consumption in public is not legal.
- Alcohol is not cheap: a beer costs on average $5.
- There are 3 brands of national beers: Stork, Flag and Casablanca.
- "Mahia" is the national liquor. It is a brandy distilled from dates or figs.

3 CLOTHING

There is no official rule on how to dress in Morocco. Although some tourists are seen wearing very short clothes, these are some guidelines:

- Dress modestly.
- Clothing that covers shoulders and knees is recommended.
- The hijab is not mandatory for women.

Contacts of interest

NUMBERS

POLICE: 112 or 190

PHYSICIAN: 141

FIREFIGHTERS: 15

ANTIVENOM (POISONOUS ANIMALS): 081 00 01 80

5. How to find the best tours

A common problem in Morocco is the low quality of paid and free tours.

RECOMMENDATIONS

- Cheap is expensive: although there are exceptions, I found the "free" tours in Morocco to be very low quality.

- Guides in Morocco must have a license to work. Don't hire "guides" who come to you out of the blue in touristic places.

- Read the tour comments carefully. Especially the negative ones. It will help you to know the problems that may happen to you.

- On some tours (especially the free ones), guides spend half of the time at "friends' craft stores". I recommend 2 things to avoid this:

  1. Read the tour reviews looking for complaints from other tourists.

  2. The most expensive tours do not usually abuse this.

CHEFCHAOUEN

Unique
Experiences

Moroccan cooking class

1.

One of the most authentic experiences in Morocco.

The cooking class begins at a local market where the ingredients for the class are purchased.

Before preparing the meal, the traditional way of preparing and drinking tea are usually shown.

Finally, traditional Moroccan dishes are prepared and tasted by the group:

- The experience lasts about 4-5 hours.
- The cities of Marrakech and Fes are the best places to take the class.

 $30-70

 FES/MARRAKECH

2.

Stay
in a Riad

I recommend that on your trip to Morocco, you stay at least once in a riad or dar.

These are traditional Moroccan houses that have been converted into hotels.

They are decorated with traditional objects and textiles. They have an interior courtyard that usually receives most of the sunlight. The larger ones have a garden, a fountain or even a swimming pool in the inner courtyard.

They are usually located in the medina of the city. They can be mainly found in the cities of Marrakech and Fes.

 $15-100

 MARRAKECH/ FES

3. **Henna Tattoo**

Henna tattoos are a way in which Moroccan women beautify their hands and feet. It is used especially in celebrations such as weddings.

Henna is a plant that comes from North Africa, Asia and northern Australia.

Please note that traditional henna has a reddish-brown color.

 FROM $5-20

 MOROCCO

It is advisable not to apply black henna as it contains chemicals that can sometimes causes allergies and leave marks for weeks.

4. Experience
a hammam

Going to a Moroccan hammam is one of the experiences in Morocco that you can't miss. What happens in a Moroccan hammam?

- First, wear a single-use piece of cotton underwear.
- The room is filled with steam and dim light.
- An employee rubs your body with a rough glove, throwing hot water on your body and applying creams and oils.

Although there are (cheaper) public hammams, it can be an uncomfortable experience if you don't understand how it works. Therefore, foreigners are recommended to go to a private one.

💰 $20-90

📍 MOROCCO

5. Climb to Africa's 2nd highest ceiling

Mount Toubkal is the highest mountain in Morocco, North Africa and the second highest on the continent (4167 m/13671 feet).

To climb to the top you need to:

- Reach the city of Imlil from Marrakech (1.5 hours).
- The ascent is usually done in 2 days.

Although it is not a very technical climb, you have to go with the right equipment. In the town of Imlil there are rental stores.

It is mandatory to hire a local guide/tour to climb this mountain.

TOUR TOUBKAL

💰 $100-200

📍 IMLIL

6. Sahara Desert
Excursion

A unique experience not to be missed in Morocco is a visit to the largest hot desert in the world: the Sahara desert.

There are options closer to Marrakech, such as a one-day tour to the Agafay desert or a 2-day tour to Zaroga.

But the most authentic activity is the desert tour in Merzouga. There you will find the largest dunes in Morocco and unlike the other 2 options, it is located in the middle of the Sahara desert.

Tours depart from Marrakech or Fes and last between 2 or 3 days.

 $100-300

 MARRAKECH/FES

7. Art class: ceramics/calligraphy

If you are passionate about arts and crafts, you have 2 great activities to do in Morocco:

- Calligraphy class: learn more about Arabic culture through writing. Learn the Arabic alphabet and ancient techniques used by calligraphy masters.

- Ceramics class: you will learn the process of making vases or sculptures.

 $35

 MARRAKECH/FES

8. Surfing

Morocco has become a trendy destination for surfers. For both experts and beginners, the country has become a must-go in the sport.

The best season for surfing is from November to March.

The most popular destinations are:

- Tahgazout/ Tamraght
- Essaouira.
- Larache.
- El Jadida.
- Safi.
- Ifni.

$20-50 CLASS

ATLANTIC COAST

9. Ski resorts

Although few associate Morocco with the sport, the country has several ski resorts.

The most famous resort is Oukaimeden, about an hour from Marrakech. You can get there by cab for about $20- 30.

Although the place falls short of European standards, it can be a unique experience since no one expects that you can ski in Morocco.

In the resort of Oukaimeden, you can find overnight accommodations.

 FROM $5-20

 MOROCCO

10. Adventure activities

For your adrenaline rush in Morocco, I recommend these 2 activities:

- Hot air balloon ride.
- Quad biking adventure in the desert.

The balloon ride usually takes place at dawn. The activity takes place through desert landscapes and palm groves. At After the activity, a traditional Moroccan breakfast is usually served.

The quad activity takes place in a desert area of the Atlas Mountains. You will also visit a small Berber village where you will you can have tea with natives of the region.

HOT AIR BALLON RIDE

QUAD

💰 FREE

📍 MARRAKECH

Best hammams

1 LES BAINS DE MARRAKECH

Private (moderate prices).

📍 Marrakech

2 HAMMAM DAR EL-BACHA

Local Hammam.

📍 Marrakech

3 HAMMAM DE LA ROSE

Local Hammam.

📍 Marrakech

4 SPA MK

Luxury Hammam.

📍 Marrakech

5 HAMMAM LES CENT CIELS

Luxury Hammam.

📍 Casablanca

6 HAMMAM SQUARE PLAZZA

Private (moderate prices).

📍 Rabat

7 HAMMAM AL JALIA

Local Hammam.

📍 Fez

8 PALAIS AMANI SPA

Luxury Hammam.

📍 Fez

9 LES BAINS MAGHRÉBINS

Luxury Hammam.

📍 Essaouira

10 HAMMAM TANJA

Private (moderate prices).

📍 Tangier

Art galleries

Morocco has a scene of local, European and American artists who have found inspiration in Morocco. These are some of the galleries you can't miss.

1 GALERIE DELACROIX
- Tangier (86 Rue de la Liberté)
- 11am-1pm, 4-9pm, Tue-Sat

2 HAMMAM DAR EL-BACHA
- Casablanca (21 Rue Abou Al Mahassine RoyaniLiberté)
- 9:30am-1pm,2:30-7pm; Mon-Sat.

3 GREEN OLIVE ARTS
- Tetouan (18 Av. Mohammed Ben Abderrahman)

4 MATISSE ART GALLERY
- Marrakech (52 Derb Aarjane, Medina)

5 DAVID BLOCH GALLERY
- Marrakech (11, Rue des Vieux Marrakchis, Gueliz)

6 GALERIE DAMGAARD
- Essaouira (G66H+MHX, Av. Oqba Ibn Nafi)

Bucket List

Do you dare to do all these experiences from my list?
Do not forget to check the boxes you complete ✓

FOOD

- Drinking mint tea with Moroccan sweets
- Eat tajine or couscous
- Taste street food

EXPERIENCES

- Relax in a hammam
- Take a cooking class
- Get a henna tattoo
- Stay in a riad/dar

SHOPPING

- Shop in a typical market without getting angry
- Buy and wear a piece of traditional Moroccan clothing

SAHARA

- Dancing at a bonfire to the rhythm of Berber music
- Watch the sunset/sunrise
- Ride a camel
- Sleep in a Berber camp

SPORTS/ADVENTURE

- Surfing
- Climb Mount Toubkal

OTHER

- Learn basic Arabic words
- Get lost at least once in the medina of Marrakech/Fes
- Take pictures in the blue streets of Chefchaouen

Historical sites

This is the list of the most memorable historical sites in Morocco. Whether for its architectural beauty, historical value or an icon of the city. The problem is that many buildings of worship are not open to non-Muslim tourists and others because they are for the exclusive use of royalty. Check off the list as many as you are able to visit.

FES

- Chouara Tannery
- Al-Attarine Madrasa

MARRAKECH

- Bahia Palace
- Majorelle Garden
- Madrasa Ben Youssef
- Secret Garden

CASABLANCA

- Hassan II Mosque

RABAT

- Hassan Tower
- Kasbah

MEKNES

- Mouley Ismail Mausoleum
- Bou Inania Madrasa

9 UNESCO SITES

- Roman city of Volubilis
- Medina of Fes
- Medina of Marrakech
- Medina of Tetouan
- City of Meknes
- Medina of Essaouira
- El Jadida
- Rabat
- Aït-Ben-Haddou

Transportation

These are the main means of transportation in Morocco: bus, cab, train, car rental and transportation. air. In this section on transportation, you can read about:

SPEED | COST
SAFETY | EASE OF USE

Transportation in Morocco

AIRLINES
Almost all of the destinations I recommend have air connections:

- <u>Rabat:</u> Rabat-Salé Airport.
- <u>Casablanca:</u> Mohammed V International Airport.
- <u>Marrakech:</u> Menara Airport.
- <u>Tangier:</u> Ibn Batouta Airport.
- <u>Fes:</u> Saïss Airport.
- <u>Agadir (30 minutes from Taghazout):</u> Al Massira Airport.
- <u>Ouarzazate (only direct connection to Casablanca):</u> Ouarzazate Airport.
- <u>Essaouira:</u> Essaouira-Mogador Airport.

*Meknes is located 76 km from Fes airport.

The 2 main airlines are:
- Royal Air Maroc.
- Air Arabia (low cost).

CHEAPOAIR
To book flights I usually use the "CheapOair" platform. What I like most about this site is that it compares flights and shows offers from airlines and travel agencies. Thus, you can find cheaper flight.

Book your flight to Morocco with CheapOair

FOR TRANSPORTION IN MOROCCO, YOU CAN USE '12GO'.
On this platform you can find all the routes and means of transport within Morocco. The page compares prices and travel time between destinations. The platform compares air, cab, bus, train and van travel.

12GO Platform

BUS
Bus transportation in Morocco is excellent: economical, safe and punctual.

- The most popular company for bus travel in Morocco is CTM: **https://ctm.ma/**
- You can also book with "Transgazhala": **https://www.transghazala.ma/**

You can also buy the ticket at the ticket office of the bus station.

*Important:
If you are traveling with a large suitcase, you have to buy an additional ticket for your suitcase at the station (5- 10 dirharms).

TAXI

These are the types of cabs in Morocco:

1) <u>Street Taxi:</u>

- For the most part, they refuse to put the meter on.
- It is recommended that you negotiate the price before getting into the cab.

2) <u>Taxi with applications:</u>

- Uber does not operate in Morocco.
- There are 2 alternatives to order a cab with an app: "Careem" and "Indriver".

3) <u>Grand cab:</u>

- These are cabs with a capacity of up to 6 persons.
- These are cabs with destination between cities (medium-long distance).
- You can either wait for the cab to fill up (economical) or pay the cab fare for 6 persons and travel alone, or with your companion.

*Advice for cabs at airports:

Scams are common with cab drivers who do not want to put the meter on or want to charge you abusive prices. So I recommend that you:

1) Ask your hotel to send you a trustworthy cab to the airport.

2) Pre-arrange the trip with 'Getyourguide'. When I am not sure about the price of the transfer from the airport, it is the service I usually use to avoid stress when traveling.

FERRY

One option to get from Spain to Morocco is by ferry. There are routes from Tangier to Barcelona, Algeciras and Tarifa. In only 1.5 hours you can cross the Strait of Gibraltar. The major companies are Balearia, GNV and FRS.

TRAINS

Trains in Morocco are punctual, cheap, fast and easily bookable. You can see the schedules, prices and book your train trip in this link: **www.oncf.ma**

The most popular routes are:

- Casablanca-Marrakech.
- Casablanca-Tangier (with stop in Rabat).
- Casablanca-Fes.
- Tangier-Fes.
- Fes-Meknes.

Seat types:

- First class.
- Second.

*Tickets are not expensive. In my opinion. It's worth buying 1st class since for little money, you get a much more comfortable seat.

There are 2 types of trains:

- <u>Al Boraq</u> (high speed train): has a route between Casablanca and Tangier, reaching speeds of up to 300 km/h (186 mph).
- <u>Al Atlas:</u> most of the connections are with this type of train.
  *In Morocco there is no subway, but there is a streetcar in Rabat and Casablanca.

CAR RENTAL

Car rental in Morocco is popular among tourists. Especially, for those who want to explore remote areas of the Atlas Mountains, go as far as the Sahara or travel along the Atlantic coast.

- Rent is about $24 on average per day.
- The cheapest companies are United Rent a Car Morocco ($6/day), Optimo Rent ($9/day) and "ADDCAR RENTAL" ($9/day).
- If you rent in advance, you will get below average prices.
- Off-airport rental locations, are 25% cheaper on average than at the airport.
- Morocco has generally good roads and you don't need 4x4 to move around the country.

Driving rules:

- The maximum speed around urban areas is 60 km/h (37 mph); outside cities, 100 km/h (62 mph), and on highways, it usually is 120km/h (75 mph).
- Depending on the company, the minimum age to rent is 18 or 21 years old.
- Driving in the right lane.

<u>**IMPORTANT**</u>

Don't forget to take photos and a video of the car before you use it in case the company tries to rip you off.

TO RENT A CAR I USE 'DISCOVER CARS'.

I usually rent on this platform since they have a wide variety of vehicles and prices. You can also see how good the vehicle is by reading reviews from past customers.

Car booking

Must Know

Money and Costs

Morocco is not expensive to travel to. It is quite a bit cheaper than traveling in Europe and similar in prices to Egypt.

The currency they use is the dirham. 10 dirhams is equivalent to 1 dollar.

Banknotes: 20, 50, 100 and 200 dirhams. Coins: 1, 2, 5 and 10 Dhs.

The dirham can be abbreviated as follows:
- MAC.
- DH.
- Dhs.

 DEBIT/CREDIT CARD
Morocco is a country where cash payment works mainly. In Morocco I could hardly pay with a card in stores, hotels, markets or restaurants.

The exception is at some of the fancier restaurants and hotels where they do accept card payment.

The card I use on my travels is from the online banks 'Wise' and 'Revolut':
- They have good exchange rates.
- You have commission-free withdrawals every month.

 TIPPING
Tipping is not mandatory in Morocco. However, it is common to tip between 5-15% in:
- Restaurants.
- To the guides and drivers on the tours.
- To workers that help you in the hotel where you stay (in elegant accommodations).

Some people recommend rounding the bill up. For example: if the meal at the restaurant is 137 dirhams, round it up to 150.

 COST FOOD AND DRINK
Eating in restaurants can go for these prices:
- Street food: $2-5.
- Mid-range restaurant: $6-15.
- Fancy restaurants: $15 and up.

These are the average prices of some items:
- Local beer (0.5 L): $4.
- Coffee: $1.5.
- Bottle of water (0.33 L): $0.35.
- Coke (0.33 L): $0.5.

 TRANSPORTATION COST
The cost of transportation in Morocco is economical:
- Airplane: internal flights usually cost between $50-100. Flying with Air Arabia is a bit cheaper than flying with Royal Air Maroc.
- Bus: traveling by bus is an economical option. Rides cost between $4-12.

- Train: train travel is usually priced similarly to bus travel ($3-10). The price of first class tickets cost a bit a bit more ($10-30).
- Taxi: traveling by cab in Morocco is cheap. Even if cab drivers ask you for 50 Dhs for a short trip, you should not pay more than 20 or 30 Dhs.

COST OF EXPERIENCES/ TICKETS

Here are some examples of the cost of tours and entrance fees to places of interest:

Marrakech
- Yves Saint Laurent Museum: $10.
- Majorelle Garden: $7.
- Bahia Palace: $7.
- Ben Youssef Madrasa: $7.

Casablanca
- Hassan II Mosque: $13.

Ouarzazate
- Atlas Studios: $6.

Tours
- Guided tour: $10-30.
- Sahara tour: $100-300.

Experiences
- Cooking class: $30-60.
- Hammam: $20-100.
- Sahara tour: $100-300.

LAUNDRY CLEANING

In Morocco I had difficulty finding an honest place to clean my clothes. In most places I was asked for $10 to clean a few items of clothing, which is way above the local price. I recommend:

1) Bargain the price by saying it's too expensive (sometimes, it worked for me).

2) Compare prices in other stores.

3) Ask your hotel for recommendations.

PRICE IN DOLLARS	LOW BUDGET	MEDIUM BUDGET	HIGH BUDGET
Lodging	8	25	90
Food	12	25	50
Transportation	2,5	5	20
Tickets and attractions	2,5	10	20
TOTAL	**$25**	**$65**	**$180**

SAVING TIPS

1 Avoid alcohol. It is one of the most expensive products in Morocco since it is not readily available.

2 Street food: although restaurants are not expensive, street stalls are very cheap (but be gentle on your stomach).

3 Renting a car in Morocco is cheap. If you are traveling with company or in a group, it will save you transportation costs.

4 Never accept the first price in the markets. You can undercut the price by less than half.

5 Beware of ATM fees: every time you withdraw money there is a $3-4 fee.

6 Travel in low season (July-August). It's extremely hot, but prices are 20% cheaper.

7 Do free visits: of the 9 UNESCO World Heritage Sites in Morocco, you only pay for Volubilis entrance.

8 Never get into a cab without agreeing on the fare or seeing the meter on.

9 If you're looking for an authentic and inexpensive experience, go to a public hammam.

Lodging in Morocco

Booking a hotel on your trip is very easy. You can find accommodation for all budgets. If you are traveling without a lot of money, you can book accommodation in hostels or hotels, which offer beds in shared rooms or private rooms for very little money.

If, on the other hand, you prefer a more comfortable place with privacy, you can book a room in a more luxurious hotel for around $120.

ONLINE BOOKING

Booking hotels is very easy. You can book several nights in a row through the internet. Reservations are only required on the following dates:

- Summer season (June-August).
- Festivities in Europe: Christmas and Easter.
- Season with the highest number of tourists: October.

HOTEL/RESORT

The destinations I describe in Morocco are very touristy. Therefore, you will find hotels for all pockets:

- Budget hotels: price between $10-30.
- Mid-range hotels: cost on average about $50.
- Fancy hotels: on average cost $120.

HOSTELS

It's the cheapest way to stay:

- You can find a bed in shared-rooms from $5.
- If you prefer to have a private room, prices range from $10 and up.
- If you are traveling alone and are eager to meet travelers, this is the best option to stay.

AIRBNB

In all of Morocco's destinations you can find accommodation through Airbnb:

- Apartment prices start at $15/night.
- In all the destinations I recommend, you can rent houses or rooms through Airbnb.

FREE ACCOMMODATION

If you want to live a different experience or travel with hardly any money, I recommend:

1) **Couchsurfing:** local travelers offer a sofa or bed in their home for free. Guests are usually great travelers looking for a cultural experience in their city.
(www.couchsurfing.com)

2) **Workaway:** an exchange of work in exchange for room and board (workaway.info).

Culture

Morocco is a country with a rich culture with many indigenous traditions. Here are some of the do's and don'ts in this country:

DO	DO NOT
Bring cash: Morocco is a country where you can hardly pay anything with a credit card.	Avoid criticizing any of these 3 topics: the king, religion or Morocco.
Cover your knees and shoulders, especially if you are a woman. Although it is not mandatory, you might feel more comfortable.	Don't greet, eat or pass things with your left hand: if you eat with Moroccans, avoid it since that hand is considered "dirty.
Get used to negotiating prices in markets: it's part of the fun in Morocco.	Do not enter mosques if you are not a Muslim. The only one that can be visited is in Casablanca (Hassan II Mosque).
Men greet each other with 2 kisses or a handshake. If you want to greet a local woman, wait to see if she will greet you.	Avoid intense displays of affection in public. It is frowned upon in Morocco.

Culture

BASIC INFORMATION

1 Arabic and Berber are the official languages of Morocco.

2 The system of government in Morocco is a constitutional monarchy. There is a multiparty system with universal suffrage in which the head of state is King Mohammed VI.

3 Morocco is located in the northwest of Africa. It is separated from Spain to the north by the Mediterranean Sea, to the east by Algeria, to the south by Western Sahara and to the west by the Atlantic Ocean.

4 The Islamic religion (99%) is the predominant religion in Morocco. Only 1% of them are Christians.

5 Morocco's population is 37 million, the capital Rabat and the most populated city is Casablanca with 3.4 million.

6 The time zone is GMT +1 and its phone code +212.

TAJINE

The tajine is the national dish of
Morocco. It takes its name from
the dish in which it is served,
a clay pot. It is simmered and
is cooked with meat, fish and
vegetables. It can also be totally
vegetarian.

Typical
dishes

COUSCOUS

One of the favorite dishes
among Moroccans, since it is
usually eaten every Friday. It is
a meal made of steamed wheat,
semolina, meat, vegetables and
chickpeas

PASTILLA

It is a traditional Moroccan cake
eaten on holidays. You can find the
meat pie chicken (traditionally pigeon
meat) or fish.

KEFTA

A Moroccan dish made of minced beef or chicken. It is usually served on skewers and is accompanied by bread and vegetables.

PASTRIES

Moroccan pastries are usually eaten with tea. Among the best known are the "chebakia", "baklava", "feqqas", "makrout" and "mhencha".

TEA

Mint or spearmint tea is the most popular drink in Morocco. It is usually served with a little sugar.

Basic words
in Arabic

Although you are not going to learn Arabic in 2 days, it is always nice to arrive in a new country and use some words in the local language. I recommend you learn some Arabic with this free app: Duolingo. You have a great variety of languages (it has helped me learn Portuguese).

GREETINGS			BASICS	
Hello	Marhaban		Thank you	shukran
How are you?	kayf halika?		You are welcome	eafwan
My name is	asmi hu		Please	min fadlik
How are you doing?	kayf halika?		Sorry	'ana asf
Good morning	sabah alkhayr		Apologies	asf
Good afternoon	masa' alkhayr		Yes	naeam
Good notches	laylat saeida		No	the

FOOD			SHOPPING	
Delicious	ladhidh		How much does it cost?	kam yukalfu?
Water	ma'		Tip	nasiha
The bill	altahqiq		I want this	arid hadha
Food	wajba		I don't want it	the 'uriduh
I am a vegetarian	'ana nabati		I like	ana yuejibuni
I am vegan	'ana nabati		Large/Small	kabirat/saghira

USEFUL			NUMBERS		
Where?	'ayn?		1	١	wahid
Bathroom	hamaam		2	٢	ithnan
Police!	shartatu!		3	٣	thalatha
Go away!	yabtaeidu!		4	٤	arba'a
Stop!	yabtaeidu!		5	٥	khamsa
It is not safe	laysat amna		6	٦	sitta
Let's go!	yallah!		7	٧	sab'a
No, thank you.	la, shukran		8	٨	thamaniya
			9	٩	tis'a

My 9
Tips

About your trip to Morocco:

1 ENJOY THE LOCAL GASTRONOMY

Don't leave Morocco without eating street food, tasting the tajine, the pastilla, the couscous, or eating typical delights while drinking mint tea.

2 TRAVEL TO MOROCCO WITH PEACE OF MIND

It is among the safest in Asia and the Middle East.

3 DON'T STRESS OUT IN THE MARKETS

Go in with the mindset that dealers are tough negotiators and that in most cases you can drop the initial price by more than half. Getting angry will only turn your enjoyment into frustration.

4 PATIENTLY CHOOSE YOUR TOURS

Many tours in Morocco are of poor quality. Read carefully the comments of former travelers to choose the tour that best suits your needs.

5 SPEND AT LEAST ONE NIGHT IN THE SAHARA

The most incredible experience Morocco has to offer. Although the desert is far from Marrakech or Fes, you shouldn't miss it!

6 IMMERSE YOURSELF IN THE LOCAL CULTURE

Take an Arabic calligraphy class, learn to make pottery, have a cooking class meal, or try to go to a hammam.

7 ALWAYS BRING CASH ON YOU

Morocco is a country where it is complicated to find places to pay by credit card.

8 BE WARY OF PEOPLE WHO ARE TOO FRIENDLY

They are most likely trying to get money out of you. Be wary when a conversation starts with "hey, friend, where are you from?

9 LOOK FOR VARIETY IN YOUR EXPERIENCES

Morocco is a spectacular country with a great variety of landscapes. Why not surf in a small village of the Atlantic, visit historical sights in the medinas of Fes or Marrakech, tour the Atlas Mountains, and get to know the Sahara?

BEST MOMENTS

10 favorite places of your trip

1 ---------------------------------

2 ---------------------------------

3 ---------------------------------

4 ---------------------------------

5 ---------------------------------

6 ---------------------------------

7 ---------------------------------

8 ---------------------------------

9 ---------------------------------

10 --------------------------------

5 favorite people you met on your trip.

1 ---------------------------------

2 ---------------------------------

3 ---------------------------------

4 ---------------------------------

5 ---------------------------------

5 foods or drinks you tried in Morocco.

1 ---------------------------------

2 ---------------------------------

3 ---------------------------------

4 ---------------------------------

5 ---------------------------------

What has been the best moment of your trip? Do you have any funny anecdotes that you will never forget? Write it down here.

Travel consulting

Would you like to plan a more customized trip?
Create another itinerary in Morocco, Vietnam, Egypt,
Colombia or other destinations? Or know how you can
permanently travel the world?

> Book a call with me at the link below
> or scan the QR code.

Acknowledgments

All of these people also helped make this book possible.

GRAPHIC DESIGN

Alejandra Sarmiento

IMAGES

Unsplash.com

iStock.com

ICONS & GRAPHICS

flaticon.com

AUTHOR OF THE GUIDE

Alberto Barambio Canet

Thank you for making it this far and for reading my Morocco travel guide. If you enjoyed the book, please leave a review on Amazon. Your opinion may help others discover this travel book. Thank you for your help!

Enjoy the trip to the fullest!

Alberto

If you want to see more about my travels, take a look at:

- ➤ LINKTR.EE/1HOURTRAVELGUIDES
- ⓘ @1HOURTRAVELGUIDES